AMERICAN SOCIETY IN WARTIME

A Da Capo Press Reprint Series

FRANKLIN D. ROOSEVELT
AND THE ERA OF THE NEW DEAL

GENERAL EDITOR: FRANK FREIDEL
Harvard University

AMERICAN SOCIETY IN WARTIME

Edited by William Fielding Ogburn

DA CAPO PRESS • NEW YORK • 1972

Library of Congress Cataloging in Publication Data

Ogburn, William Fielding, 1886-1959, ed.
    American society in wartime.

    (Franklin D. Roosevelt and the era of the New Deal)
    Original ed., issued in series: Chicago University,
Charles R. Walgreen Foundation lectures.
    Includes bibliographies.
    CONTENTS: Population, by W. F. Ogburn.–The family,
by E. W. Burgess.–The American town, by W. L. Warner.
(etc.)
    1. United States–Social conditions–1933-1945–
Addresses, essays, lectures. 2. World War, 1939-1945–
United States–Addresses, essays, lectures. I. Title.
II. Series. III. Series: Chicago. University.
Charles R. Walgreen. Foundation for the Study of
American Institutions. Lectures.
HN57.05   1972   309.1′73′0917   72-2380
ISBN 0-306-70484-6

This Da Capo Press edition of *American Society in
Wartime* is an unabridged republication of the 1943
edition published in Chicago. It is reprinted by
special arrangement with The University of Chicago Press.

Published by Da Capo Press, Inc.
A Subsidiary of Plenum Publishing Corporation
227 West 17th Street, New York, New York 10011

AMERICAN SOCIETY IN WARTIME

CHARLES R. WALGREEN FOUNDATION LECTURES

*

AMERICAN SOCIETY IN WARTIME

Edited by

WILLIAM FIELDING OGBURN

UNIVERSITY OF CHICAGO PRESS
CHICAGO · ILLINOIS

UNIVERSITY OF CHICAGO PRESS · CHICAGO 37

Agent: CAMBRIDGE UNIVERSITY PRESS · LONDON

FOREWORD

AT THE University of Chicago during the academic year 1942–43 the Charles R. Walgreen Foundation for the Study of American Institutions was privileged to sponsor three lecture series entitled "American Society in Wartime," "War and the Law," and "Medicine and the War." Each of these series will be published separately as a volume of the "Walgreen Studies in Democracy." Together they will provide a fairly comprehensive survey of the effects of the present conflict thus far upon some of the most important institutions within the United States.

This volume, like the eight others which now comprise the "Studies in Democracy," appears under the aegis of the Walgreen Foundation, but its publication has depended above all upon the generous co-operation of the authors, the editor, and the University of Chicago Press.

William T. Hutchinson, *Executive Secretary*
Charles R. Walgreen Foundation for the Study of American Institutions

PREFACE

✣

THIS volume to which these words are an introduction comprises eleven lectures delivered in the Social Science Research Building at the University of Chicago in the autumn of 1942. All but one of these papers were written by members, past and present, of the faculty of the sociology department at the University of Chicago.

The subjects on which the different lecturers presented papers were ones in which the speakers were especially competent. Each lecturer was an authority in the field which he discussed. For this reason, only a portion of our society is covered by these papers. To have dealt with the whole of society would have necessitated the co-operation of economists, political scientists, and many other specialists in our many social institutions and would have resulted in several volumes; that is, if we had adhered to the policy of having speakers deal only with their specialties. Even so, it happens that the sociologists at the University of Chicago do represent in their special interest a very wide range of social organizations and social behavior, as is shown by the chapter headings of this book.

When these lectures were begun, the United States had been in the war less than a year. For our country, therefore, the data were limited. Furthermore, the effects of the war in its later phases may be different from the beginning. For instance, the first year of the war shows a rise in the birth rate. Later in the war the births are expected to decrease. Since the United States has been in the war only a short time, other combatants that have been in longer furnish more extended data on the impact of war on our social life. The experiences of the war of 1914–18 may also be of some value to us now, for the first World War was not greatly different in some respects from the present war.

Naturally, not very much could be said about how lasting these effects of war will be. Many scars of war will remain after the armistice. On the other hand, some of our institutions will shift back to a peacetime normalcy. Such will be the case with the family, though it may be that the impetus which war gave to the employment of women outside the home will change permanently the relations within the home of a considerable number of women. Probably the greatest changes of the post-war years will be in the political and economic institutions. But what the world after the war will be like is not the subject of this volume. It concerns wartime.

Society is continually changing. At times the pace becomes very fast. The causes of these eras of rapid changes are various. We know that mechanical invention is one such cause. Note what the application of steam power to handicraft manufacture did to revolutionize the social order. A big modern war is in the same category of influences as steam and its attendant inventions. Hardly an aspect of culture escapes its influence. This volume is offered as an approach to the study of this influence. Social historians of future years will be describing the effects of this global war for many generations.

THE EDITOR

UNIVERSITY OF CHICAGO
February 9, 1943

TABLE OF CONTENTS

❋

POPULATION

WILLIAM FIELDING OGBURN

*

O BVIOUSLY wars affect population. They are fought by masses of men, and many are killed. But the effects are much more far-reaching than appear on the surface. Indeed, there is hardly an aspect of population that is not changed by war. The changes in birth rates, age distribution, migrations, and marriages that accompany and follow wars are profoundly important, too, for the welfare of society and the happiness of its members.

But we cannot always speak of war in general, for the wars of antiquity are different from modern ones in many regards. Some wars are brief; others are long and exhausting. We shall be concerned here chiefly with the present war and the war of 1914–18. Our interests are also mainly in the population of the United States and of the combatants in Europe, both allies and enemies.

DEATHS

Direct death losses in the war of 1914–18.—The proper approach seems naturally to be a consideration of deaths, which is what war means. Death is also the one exit of population from the planet and the one of two ways of reducing a population of any region.

In the war of 1914–18 the loss of life was large because many states were engaged, because the war lasted a long time, and because the weapons were highly destructive. Measures of the magnitude of the first World War and of the loss that are often quoted are sixty-five million forces mobilized by both

1

sides and thirty-five million casualties.[1] But the casualties here include the wounded and the prisoners as well as the dead. The total dying in military combat or of wounds caused thereby is the figure of loss of population directly attributable to the war. Such deaths are estimated by various authorities to total eight or ten million.[2] A loss of nine million lives because of battles in the first World War is so large that it is difficult to conceive, but there were many peoples engaged in the war—five hundred million in fact. Thus about 2 per cent of the populations of the countries engaged in the war were killed in battle or died of wounds. The war lasted on the average nearly four and a quarter years, so that the war death rate was then 0.5 per cent a year, which was a little over one-quarter of the normal death rate per year for the countries involved. In other words, the loss of life due to deaths in battles and war wounds was about one-quarter of the normal loss if the countries had not been at war.

The loss of life varied with the different countries in the war. Germany and France, as was to be expected, suffered more than England or the United States. The death rates in Germany and France were increased about 40 or 45 per cent. In Britain the increase was a little less than 35 per cent. The situation was different for the United States, where the problem of transporting soldiers and material made it more difficult to get large numbers into the battle line, as did also the lateness of entry into the war. Here the increase in the death rate was only about 6 per cent.

Deaths indirectly due to the war.—The loss by deaths in battles and of battle wounds is not the only loss of life due to war. Other deaths from war sources are epidemics, increased industrial accidents, malnutrition due to war, and military attacks

---

[1] Statistical Branch of the General Staff of the War Department.

[2] Walter Willcox, "Population and the World War," *Journal of the American Statistical Association*, June, 1923.

on the civilian population. In the latter part of the war of 1914–18 there appeared an epidemic of influenza that was very destructive of human life. It may be questioned, of course, as to whether the influenza epidemic was caused by the war. Its spread may, though, have been occasioned to a varying degree by the increased mobility of the populations meeting from various places of the earth. The loss of life from the wartime influenza was greatest in India and in Russia. Willcox has estimated that, in the world as a whole, the loss of life from epidemics was nearly the same as the loss in battle, namely, around ten million, of which seven million occurred in British India.[3] Following the influenza epidemics in Russia there was an epidemic of typhus fever which took away two million more or less.[4] After the typhus came the famine in Russia, in which the lives lost should be measured in the millions. The loss of life from influenza, typhus, and the famine probably more than doubled the death rates for a short duration of several months.

In the United States the deaths from influenza were four times as great as the number of war casualties and raised the general death rate 30 per cent. How many of these deaths are attributable to the war it is impossible to say, since we do not know whether the epidemics and famines would have occurred had there been no war. There have been famines and epidemics when there were no wars. Nor do we know how much the damage of the epidemics was furthered by the depletion of the war-torn areas. This uncertainty should not blind us, however, to the possibility of epidemics accompanying the present war.

There are civilian as well as soldier deaths from explosions in wartime, too. These deaths are due to air raids, sinking of ships, and fire from ground forces. The total deaths of civilians from such causes were probably not more than a hundred

[3] *Ibid.*   [4] *Ibid.*

thousand in the first World War and are therefore in a ratio of 1 to 90.[5]

For the war of 1914–18, then, the fair conclusion to make is that the war raised the annual death rates of the countries involved on the average 25 per cent and in the United States 6 per cent.

Deaths in the present war.—Accurate figures for deaths or for casualties are not available for the world war beginning in the summer of 1939. Up to July, 1941, when Germany attacked Russia, which may be called the first phase of the war, the losses were not so great as compared with the first two years of the first World War. Indeed, Senator Borah called it a "phoney" war during this period. The casualties were slight because Germany's mechanical preparation for war, with planes and tanks, made her victories easy against inadequately prepared adversaries. The present war is one of logistics, whereas the first World War was one of massed trench defense. What difference in loss of life the transition to a war of mobility and position with greater mechanization from one of massed positions will make, we do not as yet know. During the first phase of this present war it is estimated that Germany's losses were about one-seventh what they were in a comparable period of the first World War, that England's were probably a fifth, and that France's were one quarter.[6]

After Russia was attacked in the early summer of 1941, deaths on the European battle fronts increased greatly. The claims are quite extravagant on both sides. Thus Germany put her dead in Russia from June 22, 1941, to June 21, 1942, at 270,000, while the British estimate for the same period approximately is 2,290,000 Germans killed, dead of wounds or disease. The Russian war deaths are generally considered to

[5] Metropolitan Life Insurance Co., *Statistical Bulletin*, December, 1940.

[6] These estimates are made from material presented in the *Statistical Bulletin* of the Metropolitan Life Insurance Co. for January, 1942.

be greater. The *Statistical Bulletin* of the Metropolitan Life Insurance Company has attempted to sift out from the various claims estimates that have a much smaller margin of error. German deaths in 1942 are placed at about 500,000, with the possibility of being a hundred thousand or so more. If Germany were not at war, her dead in a year would be around 900,000. So war in 1942 probably increased her deaths by approximately 55 per cent. The same source estimates Russian military deaths in 1942 to be from 750,000 to 900,000, which is probably a slightly lower death rate per thousand population than Germany's. For other countries in 1942 the estimates of military deaths are: the United States, 11,000; the British Empire, 30,000; Italy, 30,000; Japan, 140,000–150,000; China, 100,000; and Rumania, 50,000. The total war deaths in 1942 are thus under 2,000,000 and over 1,500,000. These nations, engaged in considerable fighting in 1942, with a population of around 425,000,000, omitting China and the United States, would have lost by death 7 or 8 million if they had been at peace in 1942. Hence the war in 1942 increased the deaths by some 25 per cent, which was approximately the rate in the first World War.

Deaths to civilians as a direct result of explosions from war weapons are, of course, much greater in the second World War than in the first. This increase is due in large part to bombings from airplanes, though much destruction of civilian life by ground forces is said to have occurred in Poland and in Holland. In Great Britain during the five months following the fall of France, about 20,000 civilian deaths are recorded as the result of air raids.[7] This number is not quite one-tenth of the deaths that normally occur in Britain in five months, and thus the air raids on British cities raised the death rate for the five months of 1941 by less than 10 per cent. The ratio of the deaths to civilians by military forces was, through 1940, for

[7] *Ibid.*, December, 1940.

all states, about one for every three deaths in battle.[8] This ratio was probably greatly changed during 1941 and 1942.

Summary.—We conclude, then, with regard to direct influence of war on deaths of fighters and civilians, that the usual death rate for all the countries involved was increased around 25 per cent, that is, during the time the World War was being fought in and by the different countries; that about 40,000,000 persons would have died if there had been no war; and that, as a result of the war, about 50,000,000 died.

BIRTHS

Births are the only source for increasing the population of the world and one of two sources of augmenting the population for a region. War, in general, has the effect of slowing up this inflow of population, as would be expected when men are away from their wives and life in the army discourages marrying for young men.

War births and marriage in the United States.—However, preparation for war in the early stages may increase births. Such is the case in the United States in 1942, when the birth rate was unusually high, as is illustrated by a current story of a woman who was to meet another woman whom she did not know at the entrance to a department store. When asked how she would be recognized, the reply was: "I will be the woman who is not pregnant." It is not so much the beginning of war that increases the birth rate as it is the preparation for war, which bears a strong resemblance to the usual recovery and prosperity phases of the business cycle. In good times, especially when unemployment is greatly reduced, marriages increase, which means an increase in the birth rate. Thus the number of marriages in the United States in 1940 was 12 per cent greater than in 1939.

In the United States in 1941 and 1942, the oncoming war

[8] *Ibid.*

itself led to an increase in marriage and births, in addition to the influence of war prosperity. Thus four months before the registration under the Selective Service Act on October 16, 1940, there was a rush to the marriage-license bureaus, causing a rise at the time in the number of marriages of 15 per cent over the number in the same four months in 1939. Thus began the much-talked-of phenomenon of "war brides," for which many different reasons are given. There is about a year's lag between an increase in the marriage rate and an increase in the birth rate. Thus the birth rate in June, 1941, following the passage of the Selective Service Act in October, 1940, was 11 per cent higher than in May. This 11 per cent was in large part due to the war brides resulting from the Selective Service Act, since the normal increase in the last three years from May to June was about 2 per cent.[9]

Marriages during the war.—But, once the war is under way for a year or more, there follows a decrease in marriages and in the birth rate. Thus in France in the war of 1914–18 the marriage rate dropped from about 8 per thousand to a low of 5.1 in 1915 and to 2.3 in 1916, a reduction of 70 per cent. Germany's marriage rate was cut in half, while the low year in Italy was 60 per cent less than in normal times. In England and Wales the marriage rate was affected very much less, the lowest rate being only 10 or 12 per cent less than in normal times. Indeed, in 1915, the year after the war began, the marriage rate in England and Wales rose appreciably. The marriage rate in the United States was also not affected very much in 1918—about 10 per cent less than in 1916. The phenomena of war brides existed also in 1917 in the United States, when the marriage rate rose 6 or 7 per cent.

The birth rate during the war of 1914–18.—The course of the birth rate in the warring states in the years 1914–18 paralleled

---

[9] Harold Dorn, "The Potential Rate of Increase of the Population of the United States," *American Journal of Sociology*, September, 1942.

somewhat the course of the marriage rate, but the drop in the
birth rate was not so great as the fall of the marriage rate. In
France, for instance, the birth rate before the war of 1914–18
was about 18 or 19. It fell to 12 in 1915 and to 9.5 in 1916.
The decline in the birth rate in France was then not quite one-
half. The drop in the birth rate in Germany was about the
same as in France. In England the birth rate fell more than
the marriage rate, being about 25 per cent for the lowest year.
In the United States the fall in the birth rate was about 10 per
cent for the year 1919 as compared with 1916–17.

These declines in the birth rate mean a lessening of the inflow of population. A natural question to ask is, How much
of a reduction of the inflow of population was caused by the
war of 1914–18? In other words, if there had been no war, how
many more babies would have been born during a period of
four years, which was about the average length of the war for
all the countries involved? The problem is then to try to find
out what the birth rate would have been during the years of
the war if there had been no war. It would have been somewhat lower than the birth rate in the years of 1912–14, preceding the war, for in most countries the birth rate was falling.
If we join a line from the birth rate, in France, as an illustration in 1913–14, to what it was when the birth rate became
stable after the war and take the mid-point, we have an approximate normal birth rate for the years of the war. The
population base is not difficult to estimate, as the population
does not fluctuate violently. From the normal birth rate the
deficiency, computed by subtracting the birth rate during the
war years from the normal rate, lagged one year. Multiplying
the population by these deficiency rates for France, the product is 1,520,000 babies that would have been born had there
been no war. This deficiency in births is nearly the same as
the number of war deaths in the armed forces of France, which
was 1,358,000.

It should be noted, however, that the deficiency in births can be made up to some extent later, while, of course, there is no way of bringing back the dead soldiers. That the deficiency of births is made up in part is natural, for the soldiers who were not able to marry while they were in the trenches married in accumulated numbers after the armistice. Thus the marriage rate in France rose in 1920 to 14 and to 16 per thousand in 1921, while the normal rate was about 8 per thousand. So the birth rate also rose.

The leaders of opinion in France and other warring countries suffering heavy losses of life in battle and experiencing a huge fall in the birth rate became quite alarmed, and much was said and a little done to try to get the population to produce more babies, particularly as military prowess rests on the size of the armed forces, which in turn is dependent upon the size of the population.

In any case, the birth rate rose above normal in France in the immediate post-war years. In fact, in 1920 and 1921 the birth rate was 10 or 12 per cent higher than normal. This bulge in the birth rate in France in the second and third years after the armistice over and above the normal rate meant 200,000 more births than would normally be expected. If these 200,000 excess births are due to the war, then the deficiency in births was not so great as we at first estimated. Instead of being 1,520,000, it is fairer to estimate the number as 1,320,000 in France as a result of the war.

NATURAL INCREASE

The natural increase during the war of 1914–18.—While the loss of life in France due to war wounds, then, was 1,358,000, the loss in population due directly to the war for France was nearly twice that many. If we divide this deficiency of births in France by $4\frac{1}{3}$ years, we obtain an average fall in the birth rate of 7.6 per thousand—a war birth rate of 10.9 as compared with a normal birth rate of 18.5 per thousand.

Before the war, France's birth rate and death rate were nearly the same. This difference between the birth rate and death rate, representing the natural increase (or decrease) of population (and thus not migration), was very slight, being less than 0.5 per thousand. But during the war years this slight natural increase was turned into a natural decrease of 15 per thousand. In other words, the war meant for France, instead of a stationary population, a decreasing one at the rate of 1 or 2 (15 per thousand) persons out of every hundred per year.

In the case of Germany, in 1914, her birth rate was a good deal higher than in France, and her war-deficiency birth rate was slightly greater (9.6 per thousand deficiency). Before the war the natural increase was 8.5 per thousand per year. In Germany during the war the natural increase was turned into a natural decrease of nearly equivalent rate, that is, an excess of deaths over births of 7.9 per thousand. During the war of 1914–18 Germany's population was declining by nearly 1 per cent a year. Thus the war meant a decline in the natural increase of Germany of about 16 per thousand and in France of about 15 per thousand.

Germany and France were greatly affected by the war, but England's population growth was less affected. England's natural increase prior to 1914 showed an excess of births over deaths of 8 per thousand per year, but during the war the increase averaged 1.5 per thousand increase per year. Her population, then, did not stop growing during the war of 1914–18, despite the soldiers killed. The effect on the United States during its year and a half's participation in the war was even slighter. There was a deficiency of births for the period of 300,000—or 200,000 per year—against a normal yearly increase of 2,500,000. The deficiency in births in the United States was over twice as many as the deaths due to wounds. In the United

States the natural increase just prior to our entry into the war of 1914–18 was at the rate of 10.5 per thousand per year. But during the war the excess of births over deaths was 7.7 per thousand. The war, then, slowed up, for the duration, our natural increase by 3 per thousand.

It is too early to say what the effect of the present war will be on the natural increase of population. The birth rates of Germany and England have fallen below normal, as no doubt has that of Russia, so that there will be an increase in the death rate and a fall in the birth rate, with a consequent natural decrease of population. But how much we do not know. However, the record of the war of 1914–18 does offer some guides for surmise.

Summary on natural increase.—The war of 1914–18, in conclusion, raised the death rate 25 per cent—40 or 45 per cent for Germany and France, 30 or 35 for Great Britain, and 6 per cent for the United States. On the birth rate, the effect was to lower it about 40 to 35 per cent in France and Germany and slightly more than 7 per cent in England and a little less in the United States. The combined influence of the increase in deaths and the decrease in births was to slow up the natural growth of population, that is, the difference between births and deaths, by some 15–17 per thousand in France and Germany, by 6 per thousand in Britain, and by 3 per thousand in the United States.

AGE AND SEX

Age composition.—These shifts in birth rates and in death rates are not without effect upon the age distribution of the population. The war deaths cut down young and middle-aged men, so that immediately after the war the proportion of men in the prime of life is reduced. This fact means an increase in the proportion of older men. There is also a shortage of children, which likewise tends to increase the proportion of older men. The post-war structure, then, is fewer children and men with an increased proportion of old people.

Sex ratio.—The ratio of men to women is also affected. In fact, there were about one-fifth more women of marriageable age, fifteen to forty-four, than there were men twenty to forty-nine, in Germany, in France, and in Britain. For every 100 men there were 121 women. In Poland and Lithuania there was an excess of 40 women for every 100 men; and in Russia, an excess of 32.[10] In France, Germany, and England the war created a surplus of five million women without men of marriageable age. As a result, there was a suggestion in England for polygamy.

In the United States the war casualties amounted to only 13 out of ten thousand and was not enough to affect the sex ratio appreciably. Indeed, there was a shortage of women in the United States both before and after the war of 1917–18.

The effect of the present war on the age and sex structure will be like that of the war of 1914–18. There will be fewer children, fewer adult men, and a larger proportion of old people after the war. To what degree these changes will occur depends upon the intensity and duration of the war in each country involved.

MIGRATION

Births and deaths are not the only source of population change. Migrants come in and go out. After the war of 1914–18, there was a reduction in 1921–24 in European migration to the American countries of 40 per cent, as compared with the immigration of 1911–15.[11] This reduction in immigration was probably due to the intense nationalism developed, which set up barriers against aliens; to the depressions and lack of economic attractions; and, perhaps, to the difficulty in many

---

[10] Metropolitan Life Insurance Co., *Statistical Bulletin*, February, 1940.

[11] Imre Ferenczi, *International Migrations* (New York, 1929), I, 167.

countries of obtaining funds for moving any great distance, as from Europe to the United States. France was an exception. The reconstruction of the devastated areas called for a large labor force, and in the early 1920's France averaged 225,000 immigrants a year for five years following this war.[12] However, many were temporary dwellers, the migrants returning to Italy, Poland, and their other home countries after the areas were rebuilt. Also after the Turko-Greek War, following the war of 1914–18, there were several hundred thousands of Greeks moved from Turkey to Greece as a result of nationalistic rivalries.

In the present war there has already been some movement of peoples. The exodus from Germany has been around 300,000,[13] and more than this number from the conquered countries. At the same time there has been a controlled movement of German-speaking peoples outward from Germany and closer in toward it. The policy seems to have been to enlarge the continuous area of German-speaking peoples. Thus the Germans moved some French out of Alsace-Lorraine to make room for Germans. Similarly Poles have been transferred to other parts of Poland and Germans have moved in. In addition, Baltic, Ukrainian, and Bessarabian Germans born under other rulers have been repatriated.

Another type of population movement has been that of refugees within the borders of the same country. Thus in formerly unoccupied France the refugees were said to number two and a half million.[14] In Russia the number of refugees from conquered territory must also be very large.

A different type of transfer of peoples has been the recruiting of laborers for the German factories and fields and the use of prisoners as a labor force to take the place of the German men

[12] *Ibid.*, p. 230.

[13] Metropolitan Life Insurance Co., *Statistical Bulletin*, May, 1941.

[14] *Ibid.*

who are in other lands in a military capacity. There are probably six million such.[15]

Still another type of movement of peoples is the evacuation of cities in danger of bombing to a more scattered and safer area. In England a million people have so been moved. Though such an evacuation is temporary, the effect on the families and the children is profound.

In the United States the most notable influence of the war on population has been internal migration. The war has stirred up and mixed the population. Many millions now live in other places than they lived in the 1930's. The causes are two: the placing of young men and women in the armed forces and the movement of the working population and their families to the areas of war production and somewhat to the neighborhood of the training camps. Such areas show growths in civilian population. These migrants come from farms, towns, and cities which often show losses of population.

In general, the states that have increased in population are the southern states and those around the Great Lakes. The states that have lost are a huge block of agricultural states extending from the Mississippi to the Pacific area and extending to the southern tier of states. The states in the Northeast have, in general, also either lost or not gained much in civilian population. There are exceptions, however, to this quite general description.

With regard to metropolitan areas, the movement has been either to the highly developed manufacturing centers or to smaller manufacturing places where the growth of manufacturing has been relatively rapid during the last two decades. Some small places in manufacturing areas have also had huge growths, as have certain shipbuilding places on the water.

[15] Newspaper reports in December, 1942.

San Diego, Norfolk, Montgomery, Mobile, Washington, and Wichita have grown by a third or a quarter in two years, while the metropolitan centers of Detroit, Chicago, and Los Angeles have grown by the hundred thousands. New York City and environs, on the other hand, has lost 350,000.[16]

Farms have suffered so much loss of population that a crisis exists in the shortage of farm labor at harvest time. In 1941 the farms had a net loss of 1,350,000 population, which was twice that of 1940 and three times that of 1939.[17]

This internal migration of population has been somewhat like the movements of peoples in the upswing of economic prosperity, but to a greater degree, except that some special places have been selected for war plants and shipbuilding and that private industry would probably not have expanded very much under the normal business cycle.

After the war there will be some reversal of this movement, and after the first post-war boom the reversal will continue. The cities that had been rapidly expanding before the war will probably hold their new population better than other centers.

Conclusion.—We may observe in conclusion that there is hardly a phase of population change that is not affected by the war. In-migration and out-migration and internal distribution of population, deaths, births, age structure, and sex ratio have all changed as a result of the war effort. Our task has been to measure these changes where figures are available. The result of these measurements is to reduce somewhat the exaggerated impressions of the effects of war on population changes—exaggerated, no doubt, because war is a time for excitement and extreme statement.

[16] These statements are based upon estimates from the U.S. Bureau of the Census, made largely from rationing cards as of May 1, 1942, from a base of April 1, 1940.

[17] U.S. Department of Agriculture estimate.

BIBLIOGRAPHY

BODART, GASTON. *Losses of Life in Modern Wars, 1618–1913.* Oxford, 1916.

DUMAS, SAMUEL, and VEDEL-PETERSEN, K. O. *Losses of Life Caused by War.* Oxford, 1923.

METROPOLITAN LIFE INSURANCE Co. *Statistical Bulletins.* New York, 1940–42.

SOROKIN, PITIRIM. *Social and Cultural Dynamics.* Vol. III. New York, 1937.

THOMPSON, WARREN S. *Population Problems*, chap. iv. 3d ed. New York, 1943.

WILLCOX, WALTER. "Population and the World War," *Journal of the American Statistical Association*, June, 1923.

WRIGHT, QUINCY. *A Study of War*, Vol. II, chap. xxxi. 2 vols. Chicago, 1942.

THE FAMILY

ERNEST W. BURGESS

※

W AR, like any other crisis, has its obvious, although more superficial, and its subtler, but more profound, effects upon the family. The impact of war upon the family is readily observable in its surface manifestations, and these can be stated in part quantitatively. They are not to be thought of as unimportant in themselves, but they acquire added meaning to the extent that they can be related significantly to long-time trends. These external effects will be briefly summarized, preliminary to an attempt to discover in so far as feasible the more basic changes taking place under the impact of war upon the modern American family.

OBSERVABLE CHANGES

Certain effects of war upon the family flow, first of all, from the withdrawal of millions of young men from civilian to military life. Recent estimates give approximately five and one-half million as the number of men now in the armed forces.[1] This number is to be doubled by the end of 1943. These men are largely but not entirely single and mainly in their twenties or early thirties. The great majority have been taken out of families in which they were reared and required to make adjustment to the Army-camp situation. These adjustments are none too easy for those who have been sheltered or for certain types of personality. An extreme illustration is that 57,000, or 2.85 per cent, of the first two million regis-

[1] As of December, 1942.

trants who were examined for induction into the Army under the Selective Training and Service Act of 1940 were rejected for mental and nervous disorders serious enough to disqualify a man for military service.[2]

This withdrawal of men from the primary group controls of the home and of the neighborhood removes restraining influences against socially disapproved forms of behavior. Drinking, gambling, prostitution, and illicit sex behavior in past wars have been higher among men in military than in civilian life.[3] In this war unusual efforts have been made by the Army and by civilian organizations to counteract the influences predisposing to irregular conduct.[4] The Division of Special Services of the Army provides education and recreational activities, including radio and motion-picture programs for men in Army camps. The United Service Organizations, a joint effort of character-building agencies and other individual groups, have established recreational centers in communities near Army camps to furnish wholesome activities for men on leave. Preventive and repressive measures have also been taken by the Army, by the National Advisory Police Committee on Social Protection, by local citizens' committees, and by police departments to control drinking, gambling, and prostitution. The net result seems to be that "no American Army in all history has been so orderly" and that it is "more orderly than any other present army."[5]

[2] American Youth Commission, *Youth and the Future* (Washington, D.C.: American Council on Education, 1942); cf. also L. G. Rowntree, K. H. McGill, and O. H. Folk, "Health of Selective Service Registrants," *Journal of the American Medical Association*, CXVIII (April 4, 1942), 1223–27.

[3] Willard Waller, *War in the Twentieth Century* (New York: Random House, 1940), pp. 490–94, and J. H. S. Bossard, "War and the Family," *American Sociological Review*, VI (June, 1941), 336–37.

[4] Fred K. Hoehler, "Services for Men in the Armed Forces," *Social Service Review*, XVI (September, 1942), 389–400.

[5] "Survey of Army Camp Drinking" (Office of War Information News Release, No. 1020) (published in daily newspapers, December 30–31, 1942).

The survey of drinking conditions in and around Army camps made by the Office of War Information indicated that

there is not excessive drinking among the troops, and drinking does not constitute a serious problem; that the sale of 3.2 beer in the post exchanges in training camps is a positive factor in Army sobriety . . . . ; [that] there is no indication that the sale of beer lowers the number of total abstainers; [and that] there seems to be a definite correlation between adequate recreational facilities and soldier sobriety.[6]

Strenuous efforts have been made to combat venereal diseases, which seriously impair the physical efficiency of our armed forces, both by suppressing commercial prostitution through the action of federal and local agencies[7] and by penalties for the nonuse of prophylactics by the soldier. Repressive measures as now planned are more far-reaching than ever before. A statement upon the report of the enforcement section of the National Advisory Police Committee on Social Protection summarizing accomplishments outlines the future program:

Having closed "red light" districts in approximately 350 cities and towns the police officials and sheriffs are now concentrating on the prostitutes operating outside of the segregated districts. This group includes the street walker, the call-girl, and the non-commercial girl who is promiscuous with men in uniform. . . . . It has been found effective for enforcement officers to meet with hotel managers, taxicab owners, tourist camp operators, and tavern owners, to explain the need for their cooperation in the enforcement program.[8]

As a result of these different activities, the incidence of venereal diseases in the Army has been kept under control. There was indeed a sharp rise in Army rates of infection from venereal diseases from 29.6 per thousand in 1939 to 42.5 in

[6] *Ibid.*

[7] See "Police Officials from 15 States Confer with Federal Leaders on Social Protection," *Victory*, III, No. 27 (July 7, 1942), 28.

[8] *Victory*, III, No. 52 (December 29, 1942), 22.

1940.[9] The effect of concerted recreational, protective, and repressive measures was shown, however, by a decline from 40.5 per thousand men for 1941 to 38 for the first six months of 1942.[10]

The statistical evidence of a higher incidence of irregular sexual contacts in Army than in civilian life is based upon a comparison of venereal infection rates found in registrants examined by local Selective Service boards and those reported from Army camps. One study of 19,923 registrants examined by local boards gives a rate of 34.9 per thousand men,[11] which compares with the Army rate of 42 during a similar period. Taking into account the more general use of prophylactic measures in the Army, it seems fair to make the inference that greater sexual promiscuity exists in the military than in the civilian community.

No quantitative data are available to show whether drinking and gambling are greater, the same, or less in military than in civilian life in this war. Reports from observers seem to indicate that these, as well as sexually irregular conduct, are less than in American armies in the past,[12] in part because of the all-round preventive and repressive program of military and civilian effort. The data indicating that these forms of conduct are probably more frequent in Army than in civilian life come from letters and statements from soldiers and sailors.[13] Such findings are in conformity with the sociological theories

[9] *Journal of the American Medical Association*, CXVIII (March 7, 1942), 824.

[10] Statement by Secretary of War Stimson, *New York Times*, September 18, 1942, p. 13.

[11] Rowntree, McGill, and Folk, *op. cit.* In England an increase of 12.5 per cent of new infections with syphilis is reported for 1940 over 1939 in the civilian population, which rises to an increase of 23 per cent if men in the army are included (*Journal of the American Medical Association*, CXIX [May 30, 1942], 431).

[12] The rate of venereal infection was 101.9 per thousand men in World War I (*Report of the Surgeon General of the U.S. Army, 1919*, Part I, pp. 955–59).

[13] See John F. Cuber, "The College Youth Goes to War," *Marriage and Family Living*, Vol. V (February, 1943).

of expected behavior in a male community and of mobility as a factor undermining primary social control and conduct.

These types of behavior as antithetical to familism may perhaps also be taken as an index of the degree to which military life unfits men to resume their places in the family after the war. Here, however, we are dealing with a rather complicated balance of forces making for and against domesticity. To the great majority of men the war is a disagreeable job to be finished as soon as possible in order to return to civilian life, to settle down, and to enjoy home comforts, all the more attractive by contrast with the Army camp. Then, too, the discipline of the Army, the regularity of its routine, and the opportunity to learn a trade are valuable experiences for civilian readjustment to many previously unemployed youth of the depression decade.

The second evident effect of the war upon the family is the entrance of women into war and civilian industry to replace men drawn into the armed forces. The ten and one-half million women in the labor force in November, 1940, rose to fifteen million three hundred thousand in November, 1942.[14] Chairman McNutt of the War Manpower Commission stated that, at the beginning of 1943, four million women were working in war plants out of a total war labor force of seventeen and a half million and that by the end of this year they would number six million out of over twenty million.[15] The percentage of women of all workers in metal-working industries engaged in production of aircraft, tanks, guns, and other munitions rose from 9.4 in October, 1941, to 16.5 in November, 1942.[16]

The vast exodus of young men from the home into service and the upsurge of women in industry cannot but have reper-

[14] U.S. Bureau of the Census, *Victory*, December 22, 1942, p. 5.

[15] Office of War Information, *Information Digest*, No. 636, January 9, 1943, p. 2.

[16] *Victory*, January 6, 1943, p. 18 (data of War Production Board).

cussions in the home. First to be evident are reports from all over the country of neglect of small children, locked in the house, the apartment, or the trailer during the hours the mother is employed in war industry. The need of remedying this neglect is now so evident that private and public efforts are being made to meet it. Although the United States has been in the war little more than a year, signs are multiplying that an increase in juvenile delinquency is already in the making. The experience of other countries, as well as the United States, in World War I indicates that the marked increase in juvenile delinquency does not come until the second year of war. Delinquency rates in England are now reported as approximately 40–50 per cent higher than in the pre-war years.[17] Scattered reports from this country indicate that rates are stationary in some communities and even declining in others,[18] but large cities like Chicago,[19] Los Angeles,[20] and New York[21] have experienced small increases in youthful crime. There seems little doubt that the removal of the father, and more often the older brother, from the home and the absence from the family of the mother or older sister during work will result in a piling-up of juvenile offenses during 1943. Charles L. Chute, executive director of the National Probation Association, reports, upon the basis of a nation-wide survey of cases in juvenile courts in 128 cities or counties of 50,000 population or over, an increase in delinquency of 9 per cent in 1942 over 1941.[22]

[17] Eleanor T. Glueck, "Wartime Delinquency," *Journal of Criminal Law and Criminology*, XXXIII (July-August, 1942), 119–35.

[18] W. C. Reckless, "Impact of War on Crime, Delinquency, and Prostitution," *American Journal of Sociology*, XLVIII (November, 1942), 384.

[19] Increase 3.8 per cent in complaints to police, first nine months 1942 over 1941.

[20] Increase 4.8 per cent in juvenile court cases, first six months 1942 over 1941.

[21] Increase 10.8 per cent in cases in children's court 1942 over 1941.

[22] "The Facts on War-Time Delinquency and Their Significance," *Marriage and Family Living*, V (May, 1943), 25. For further discussion of juvenile delinquency in war see the chapter on "Crime" by E. H. Sutherland in this volume.

MARRIAGE, DIVORCE, AND BIRTHS

The effects of the war upon marriage are already evident. "The 1941 marriage rate—12.6 per 100,000 population—was the highest rate ever recorded in the United States."[23] The increase in marriages as affected by the war began in 1940, preceding and following the passage of the Selective Service Act in September of that year. There is every reason to believe

TABLE 1

VARIATIONS IN THE MARRIAGE RATE IN WORLD WAR I COMPARED
WITH ACTUAL CHANGES IN THE MARRIAGE RATE IN
WORLD WAR II

TIME IN REFERENCE TO THE WAR	WORLD WAR I		WORLD WAR II	
	Year	Marriage Rate per 1,000	Year	Marriage Rate per 1,000
Pre-war year..........	1916	10.6	1939	10.5
Selective Service........	1917*	11.1	{1940	11.9†
			1941	12.6
War years..............	1918	9.7	1942—	....
First post-war year......	1919	11.0	....	....
Second post-war year....	1920	12.0	....	....
Third post-war year.....	1921	10.7	....	....

* In 1917 the draft law was passed after war was declared in April.

† In 1940 the long discussion of the Selective Service Act affected marriage rates as early as June, although it was not passed until September.

that the change in the marriage rate during this war will follow the pattern of World War I, as indicated in Table 1. The marriage rate rises before and during the early period of the entrance of men into the armed forces, declines during the year or years of war, increases during the first two post-war years, and then returns to normal in the third post-war year.

The first phase of the marriage cycle as affected by the war reached its climax in the increases of the marriage rate in 1941 and the early months of 1942 and these may be expected to fall

[23] Quoted from release by the Bureau of the Census, July 17, 1942, and estimated on basis of reports from eighteen states with central registration systems.

off somewhat during the remainder of 1942. The increase was largely due to hasty and hurried-up marriages. Hasty marriages are of three types: first, there are those entered into on short acquaintance to avoid Selective Service; second, there are the war-camp marriages, typically of the homesick soldier or sailor and of the girl attracted by the glamour of the uniform; and, third, there are the romantic marriages of the men in the expeditionary forces, meeting and falling in love with and marrying Australian, Irish, and English girls. These last, however, do not appear in United States marriage reports, since the weddings take place in foreign countries.

That marriage rates should begin their decline in 1942 and decrease still further in 1943 results from postponed unions. These held-over marriages are of two kinds, voluntary and involuntary. Many young people moved more by prudential than romantic reasons have decided to wait until the war is over to marry. Some of these weddings will never take place, either because one or the other will change his mind or because the young man will die or be incapacitated for marriage. As numerous, perhaps, are the involuntary postponed marriages. The great majority of men not engaged before entering the service are disposed to remain single until their return after the war.

World War I was of short duration. The number of casualties in the Army during the eighteen months of war was only 50,510 killed and 182,674 wounded.[24] Although the number of casualties in the first year of the present war is relatively small (58,307, of whom 8,192 are known to be killed, 6,335 wounded, and the remainder reported as prisoners or missing), the probabilities are that they will considerably exceed those of 1917–18, as the American expeditionary forces move into action on all continents.

The sum total of men killed, of those surviving but incapaci-

[24] The deaths in the Navy during 1917–18 were only 871.

tated for marriage, and of those marrying foreign brides will undoubtedly increase the number of American young women of this generation destined to remain single. How great this problem will ultimately become is, of course, contingent upon the duration of the war and the extent and degree of American participation in it.

The divorce rate typically declines during war.[25] Many men temporarily solve their marital difficulties by enlisting. Marriages on the brink of disaster will be saved "for the duration" by the husband entering the armed forces through Selective Service. Wives who otherwise might sue for separate maintenance or divorce postpone such action until after the war, a prudential course in view of compulsory allowances to dependents of men in the service. Then, too, divorces are more difficult to obtain when the husband is a soldier, sailor, or aviator.

The deficit in divorces during the war is certain from past experience to be more than made up after the war.[26] The higher proportion of unhappy unions arising from hasty marriages to avoid Selective Service, in war camps, and abroad, and, to a lesser degree, those resulting from hurried-up unions, will contribute to the upswing in the divorce rate. Also to be included are the divorces due to all the factors which cause husband and wife to grow apart during their enforced separation.

The effects of the war upon marriage have their inevitable effect upon the birth rate. In World War I the birth rate was nearly as high for the years 1917 and 1918 as for the pre-war year 1916. The pre-war year of 1940, with a higher birth rate (17.9) than any year since 1931, was outdistanced by 1941

[25] The war year 1918 showed a sharp decline in divorce rates according to data reported from all New England states except Maine (see Metropolitan Life Insurance Co., "Trend of Divorce in Fifty Years," *Statistical Bulletin*, XX [February, 1939], 1-2).

[26] The post-war years 1919 and 1920 had extraordinarily high divorce rates (*ibid.*).

(18.9), which in turn is expected to yield to 1942 (21.0) as the banner year for births. The high rate for 1941 was largely due to the sharp rise in the marriage rate in 1940, which, continuing in 1941, was largely responsible for the anticipated exceptionally high 1942 birth rate. Contributing to the high rates of 1941 and 1942 was the decision of an undeterminable number of previously childless couples to have a child as a ground for escape of the husband from Selective Service.

TABLE 2

VARIATIONS IN THE BIRTH RATE IN WORLD WAR I COMPARED
WITH ACTUAL AND EXPECTED CHANGES IN THE BIRTH RATE
IN WORLD WAR II

TIME IN RELATION TO THE WAR	WORLD WAR I		WORLD WAR II	
	Year	Birth Rate	Year	Birth Rate
Pre-war year...........	1916	25.0	1940	17.9
First year of draft.......	1917	24.7	1941	18.9
First full-year war......	1918	24.6	1942	21.0*
Second full-year war.....	....	....	1943†	....
First post-war year......	1919	22.3	....	....
Second post-war year....	1920	23.7	....	....
Third post-war year.....	1921	24.2	....	....
Fourth post-war year....	1922	22.3	....	....

* Although 1943 is the second full war year, it may be the first to show a decrease in the birth rate, which will be more marked for 1944.

† Estimate in Metropolitan Life Insurance Co., "No Shortage of Babies during Our First Year of War," *Statistical Bulletin*, XXIII (December, 1942), 42.

Owing to the withdrawal of a million men during 1942, the birth rate should show a moderate decline for 1943 and, with other millions overseas in the next year, a rather marked decrease for 1944. A recovery in the birth rate cannot be expected upon the basis of experience in World War I until the second and third post-war-year periods. This expected continued increase in the birth rate in the third post-war year may be reversed if economic conditions in the previous years are bad.

If there is an increase of irregular sexual intercourse of men in the armed forces and of single and married women, the illegitimate birth rate and the abortion rate may both be expected to rise.

LONG-TIME CHANGES

These changes already noted, while interesting and important, should not blind us to the more fundamental transformations in family structure, functions, and relationships which have been in process for decades. The impact of the war, like that of any other crisis, tends to speed up these changes rather than to reverse them or to introduce new trends. Social scientists should, therefore, always be on their guard against the common-sense fallacy of assuming that a given reversal of a trend, due to temporary wartime conditions, is indicative of a permanent change. It is only wishful thinking to project beyond the wartime emergency the revival of neighborliness among urbanites now evidenced in sharing automobiles or in Civilian Defense block activities. Nor does the present tendency of many war brides to reside with their parents or parents-in-law forecast a trend after the war to increased control of the kinship group over the young couple after marriage.[27] Aside from these and other temporary reversals, the safest forecast of the future is to project past trends into the future unless some counteracting factor is clearly evident.

FAMILY ORGANIZATION

The changes now taking place in family organization may best be seen in their long historical perspective and in relation to two contrasting types of family structure. Let us assume that the complete subordination of the individual to the fam-

---

[27] A similar tendency in the depression had no lasting effect. A well-to-do widow remarked: "I think the depression is fine. I have not been so happy in years. My son and son-in-law both lost their jobs and they and their wives are living with me. I have my children home again."

ily, on the one hand, and the fullest self-expression of its individual members compatible with the continued existence of the family, on the other, represent the two extreme constructions.

Of the historical and existing types of families, the large patriarchal family most closely approximates the type of the institutional family where the individual members of the small family unit are completely subordinated to the interests of the large family. The modern American family residing in apartment-house areas of the city approximates nearest to the type of family in which the members have full freedom of self-expression. The two contrasting types will be named the "institutional" and the "companionship," since the first emphasizes subordination to social control and the second stresses the interpersonal basis of modern matrimony.

A summary comparison of the historical approximations of these two types will indicate the point-by-point outstanding differences between the small family unit of husband, wife, and children with subordinate position of the members in the large patriarchal family and their individualization in the modern family.

The patriarchal family was authoritarian and autocratic, with power vested in the head of the family and with the subordination of his wife, sons, and their wives and his unmarried daughters and children to his authority; the modern family in its ideals is democratic, based on equality of husband and wife, with consensus in making decisions and with increasing autonomy with age of children. Marriage is arranged by parents in the patriarchal family with emphasis upon prudence, upon economic and social status, and upon adjustment of the son-in-law or daughter-in-law to the family group. Marriage is in the hands of the young people in the modern family, and the selection is on the basis of romance, affection, and personality adjustment to each other. Compliance with duty and the following of tradition are guiding principles of the patriarchal family; the achievement of personal happiness and the desire for innovation are watchwords of the modern family. The chief historic functions of the family—economic, educational, recreational, health, protective, and religious—were found in their fullest development in the large patriarchal family of ancient Israel, Rome, and Greece and are still prevalent in this familial type in the village communities of China, India, and Japan. These historic functions have largely departed from the modern urban family. One example is sufficient to illustrate the vast extent of this change. All members of the large patriarchal family were employed in home industry, both for production and for consumption; husband and wife in the modern urban family of the apartment-house district of the large city are typically employed outside the home, with a resulting diminution of its economic function.

For decades the American family has been evolving from a semipatriarchal type revolving around the father and husband as head and authority to the democratic type based upon consensus in making decisions, upon the conception of the equality of husband and wife, and upon the growth of autonomy with age of the children. Accompanying this evolution has been the decreasing size of the family, the diminishing control of the kinship group and of the community over the small family unit, and a growing sense of its independence. The external factors making for family stability, such as control by custom and community opinion, have been greatly weakened. The permanence of marriage is more and more dependent upon the tenuous bonds of affection, temperamental compatibility, and common interests.

Although the democratic conception is accepted in principle as the basis of the American family, it is still far from being realized. This retardation in the translation of theory into action is partly the result of immigration with its transplanting to the New World of the Old World semipatriarchal family. But it is much more the reflection of the ambivalent role of women in American culture.

Pearl S. Buck, in her recent book *Of Men and Women*, analyzing the American scene with the objectivity of the "sociological stranger" from the vantage point of comparison with recent Chinese developments, seeks to explain the contradiction between the apparent opportunity of American women and the paucity of their achievements. She attributes it to the human failing of "wanting to eat one's cake and have it too." Women prize the outward symbols of equality but are not willing to relinquish the privileges of "the angel upon the pedestal" required by the struggle in the real world of achievement. Men, sustained by an inner conviction of superiority, graciously grant them the show rather than the substance of equality. The business or professional success of the husband is still paraded to the world by the conspicuous leisure of his wife.

One phase of this ambiguity in husband-wife relations, the nominally equal but really inferior status of the wife, is often of decisive importance for success or failure in marriage. The husband may assume a position of dominance in family relations, relegating the wife to a subordinate position. Or, conceiving the home to be the domain of the woman as business is that of the man, he may withdraw as entirely as possible from what he considers the lesser responsibility of the household and of the rearing of children.

What, in the light of this analysis, will be the effect of war upon the American family? Without doubt, the trend to the companionship type of family characterized by equality of the sexes and democratic procedures in the home will continue with a new momentum under the impetus of the wartime situation.[28]

[28] Pearl S. Buck is apprehensive of the effect upon human relations if women greatly outnumber men after the war. She says: "If many women compete with each other for

The biggest change to be anticipated is a further rise in the status of women. World War I gave women the outward symbols of equality with men; namely, the suffrage and a social freedom permitting short skirts, bobbed hair, drinking, and smoking. Abolished also along with the open notorious "red-light" districts was the caste of the prostitute and the rigid line of differentiation between respectable and disreputable women.[29]

The present war and the following reconstruction period bid fair to give women more of the substance of equality than did the last conflict, in part because of its expected longer duration. The formation of the Army and Navy auxiliary corps of women—the WAAC's and the WAVE's—is symbolic of the new role conceded to women. Women are being given jobs both in military and in civilian industry previously filled only by men. The big increase in the number of working women spells increased economic independence which lays a solid basis for enhanced social status.

This increase in economic independence will be reflected in the more secure position of equality of women in the home. In fact, the absence of husband and father in the Army or in a distant munitions industry will also give many wives a larger role of management in the home, at the same time decreasing the sense of family responsibility on the part of the man.

FAMILY FUNCTIONS

The changes taking place in familial functions for the period 1900–1929 have been described in convincing detail by W. F. Ogburn and Clark Tibbitts in *Recent Social Changes* and need here be only summarized. The family has lost or is losing its

a few men, ... the place and power of men will be exalted out of all proportion, and we shall eventually have a fascist relationship between men and women" (*American Unity and Asia* [New York: John Day Co., 1942], p. 111).

[29] Walter C. Reckless, *Vice in Chicago* (Chicago: University of Chicago Press, 1933), pp. 57–58.

historic functions of economic production for the market and for home consumption, care of health, education of its members, protective activities, recreation, and religious rites in the home. The intrinsic functions remaining with the family are the giving and receiving of affection by its members, the bearing and rearing of children, and their informal education. The big surge of women into industry in wartime certainly means further curtailment of economic activities in the home, more reliance upon other institutions for health needs, a great expansion in day nurseries for the care of young children, more dependence upon recreational facilities outside the home, and less time for the mother to give to the educational and religious development of her children.

Of these shifts, the expansion of day nurseries is perhaps the most significant, since this involves the transference in large part of a so-called "intrinsic" function of the family—rearing of the preschool child—outside the home. Up to now nurseries have been limited to the care of the small children of the well-to-do and of the poorest parents. Now proposals are on foot greatly to extend these facilities for the day care of children of working mothers.

There seems little doubt that this expansion of day nurseries will continue after the war, although there may be a recession in the immediate post-war period to the degree that married women will be compelled to surrender their jobs to men. But, in the longer perspective of the future, day nurseries are destined to become as necessary and as public a function as the public schools. The advocates of day nurseries claim that, in addition to the affectional care of its parents, the child needs the socializing influence of its age group which is not satisfactorily achieved in one- and two-child families and not always realized in those of larger size, where large age differences between children result from the spacing commended by advocates of planned parenthood.

The loss by the family of its historic functions greatly increased its economic insecurity. With the exhaustion of free land, private charity was largely relied upon to relieve the distress caused by the exigencies of death, accidents, sickness, and unemployment. Although the movement for governmental intervention to deal with these problems was well under way before the thirties, the crisis of the last great financial depression finally brought about a merger of projects and proposals into a federal system of social security. The families of workingmen are now safeguarded by compensation insurance and pension against the contingencies of accident, unemployment, and old age. Most significant, perhaps, for the small family unit is the provision of pensions for the aged which permits them to live in some degree of independence and relieves their children of responsibility for their support.

The war is likely further to augment governmental provision for the security of the family. The White House Conference on Children in a Democracy, 1939–40, devoted four of the eleven sections of its report to the family. The Family Security Committee, established in the Office of the Director of Defense, Health and Welfare Services and composed of representatives of voluntary as well as governmental effort, is concerned with safeguarding the values of family life during the period in which the United States is engaged in war. It has first centered its attention upon the strengthening of governmental social services in the field of family security.

FAMILY RELATIONS

Under the term "family relations" will be considered the effects of the war upon the personal interaction of the members of the family. Changes in progress in their interrelationships are to be seen in the context of the family conceived of not as an institution but as a unit of companionship and of the function of the family as inhering in supplying its members with affection, intimate appreciation, and emotional security. Whatever interferes with the adequate discharge of this function—as temperamental incompatibility, lack of common interest, and disparity in ideals and values—is disruptive of family unity.

Present-day attitudes toward sex and marriage are powerfully affected by the urban way of life, with its high valuation of rational, standardized, and sophisticated behavior. Corresponding to this shift from rural to urban attitudes are three changes in sex mores which should be specifically mentioned. They all received an impetus from the conditions associated with World War I and are all quite certain to be further affected by the progress of the present conflict.

The lifting of the taboo upon sex and the growth of the movement of sex instruction of children and youth accelerated by World War I will receive a further push forward from this war. The social hygiene lectures and the compulsory use of prophylaxis familiarized the soldiers and sailors of World War I with the methods of birth control, lessons that will be repeated for the larger armed forces of this war.

The increase of premarital intercourse following in the wake of World War I, which was accelerated by the depression, appears likely to be further augmented by various conditions accompanying this war, as glamour of the uniform, patriotic justification in acceding to the desire of a man about to give his life for his country, and the declining value of virginity and chastity.[30]

In the code of sophisticated modern young people the lessening value placed upon chastity does not carry with it the approval of promiscuity. Sexual intercourse is regarded as a privilege of engagement, as permissible when a couple are in love, and to be condoned under certain other circumstances. But

[30] See Lewis M. Terman, *Psychological Factors in Marital Happiness* (New York: McGraw-Hill Book Co., 1938), pp. 319–24.

promiscuity of the young woman and, to a lesser degree, of the young man draws group disapproval. This code of modern youth seems likely to be extended rather than restricted under conditions of wartime. The double standard of morals is well on its way out. Moralists still striving to maintain the value of chastity are losing the full force of their stock arguments, namely: the fear of pregnancy, now diminished by the use of contraceptives, and the danger of venereal infection, now lessened by preventives and prophylaxis and by the discovery of chemical and fever treatments for syphilis and of sulfathiasol cure for gonorrhea.[31]

Upon this background of changing sex mores may be sketched the modifications of family relations which will probably result from the impact of war.

The decline in the restraining influence of parents upon young people, in conjunction with other factors, is making for a higher proportion of war marriages during this than in the preceding war. These comprise not only hurried-up but hasty unions, as marriages to avoid Selective Service, war-camp marriages, and marriages of enlisted men in expeditionary forces abroad. The romantic impulses of youth, freed from the prudential restraint of their elders, will lead to many marriages upon short acquaintance, slight knowledge of each other, and insufficient provision for the economic and emotional security of the wife. A high proportion of these unions is certain to turn out unhappily, as indicated by studies of the adverse relation between short acquaintance and adjustment in marriage. Separation while the husband is in the armed forces will also be a disruptive factor, especially upon unions where intercommunication has been insufficient to provide the sharing of experiences and common understanding of feelings, attitudes, and ideals essential to a durable relationship.

[31] John H. Stokes, M.D., "The Wartime Control of Venereal Disease," *Journal of the American Medical Association*, CXX (December 5, 1942), 1093-99.

During the war all American families are likely to be under considerable stress and strain. There is the shock occasioned by bereavement due to the loss in line of duty of a son, husband, or father. There is the painful readjustment of the wife and other relatives to the serviceman returning with physical or mental handicap.

Then, too, wartime is already bringing other sudden changes that are disquieting and disrupting. There is mass migration of families and individuals to war-boom communities. Millions of families on stationary incomes already feel the pinch of advancing prices and taxes and are fearful of the menace of inflation. But families with members employed in war industries are experiencing big jumps in income. Both sudden depression and quick prosperity confront the family and its members with changes in habits, attitudes, and roles which contribute to its instability.

A counteracting factor favorable to family stability is the unifying influence of the sense of participation in the national effort, all the more because of the sacrifices entailed. The balancing of these factors in individual cases requires discrimination between those families which adjust well and those which adjust badly to the wartime situation.

Owing to the research of Angell, Bakke, Cavan and Ranck, and Komarovsky upon the effect of the depression upon the family, findings are available which enable us to predict with some assurance the probable consequences, favorable or unfavorable, of any other crisis such as that of war upon the family according to its type of internal organization.[32]

[32] R. C. Angell, *The Family Encounters the Depression* (New York: Charles Scribner's Sons, 1936); E. W. Bakke, *Citizens without Work* (New Haven: Yale University Press, 1940); Ruth S. Cavan and Katharine R. Ranck, *The Family and the Depression* (Chicago: University of Chicago Press, 1938); Mirra Komarovsky, *The Unemployed Man and His Family* (New York: Dryden Press, 1940); S. A. Stouffer and Paul Lazarsfeld, *Research Memorandum on the Family in the Depression* (New York: Social Science Research Council, 1937).

Angell's findings are particularly valuable because he identified two variables—integration and adaptability—as significantly related to the capacity of the family to withstand and adjust to marked financial reverses. The more integrated and adaptable families were better able to meet them, in general, than were the less integrated and less adaptable families. A restudy of these cases now under way for the Committee on Appraisal of the Social Science Research Council arrived at the interesting conclusion that adaptability of the family was more important than its integration for its readjustment to the depression.[33]

In the past, when the unity of the family was insured by its institutional functions and by close community control, the integration of its members was probably much more important than their adaptability. With the transition to the companionship type of family relations, and especially in a time of crisis, adaptability becomes more important in adjustment than integration. In fact, while moderate integration may be helpful in adjustment, too high as well as too low integration may hamper the changes in habits and roles essential for meeting crisis conditions.

THE FAMILY AFTER THE WAR

The war, then, will bring great stresses upon marriage and the family, increasing its instability. As an index of this, divorce will markedly increase after the war, an increase that will continue at least for some years, with a higher rate than the present one divorce for every six marriages.

Ten years ago a statistician projecting into the future the divorce rate, which since the Civil War has been increasing at the rate of 3 per cent a year, figured that by the year 1965 there would be one divorce for every two marriages.[34] Other writers

[33] Unpublished manuscript on "Repetitive Studies."

[34] Alfred Cahen, *Statistical Analysis of American Divorce* (New York: Columbia University Press, 1932).

not statisticians, observing concrete evidences of family instability and unhappiness, have predicted the actual disappearance of the family. Will the war, by increasing family instability, hasten the time of its passing? In reply to these gloomy
prophecies certain considerations may be advanced.

1. The companionship family still retains the intrinsic and
essential functions of the family, namely, the giving and receiving of affection, the bearing and rearing of children, and
the guidance of their personality development. It is likely to
endure because it is better able to discharge these functions
than was the institutional family.

2. Since World War I many services for the family have orig-
inated or have been further developed, such as family social
work, maternal and child health, child guidance, social security, child study, home economics, legal aid for families,
associations for family living, education for family life, and
marriage and family counseling. These agencies are keenly
alive to the effect of wartime conditions upon the family and
are actively engaged in taking measures to deal with them.
They are orienting their activities to assist in the transition
from the institutional to the companionship family.

3. Family instability is essentially a phenomenon of the
transition from the institutional to the companionship type of
family. The effect of a crisis like war is both to accelerate the
transition and to introduce temporary disrupting conditions.

The solution of the present problem of family instability
accentuated by wartime conditions is not the setting-up of
some new form of the institutional family, as advocated by
Professor P. A. Sorokin and others.[35] It is rather to recognize
the trend to the companionship family and to take those

[35] *The Crisis of Our Age* (New York: E. P. Dutton & Co., 1941), p. 203; see also C. C.
Zimmerman and Merle Frampton, *Family and Society* (New York: D. Van Nostrand
Co., 1935), and Clifford Kirkpatrick, *Nazi Germany: Its Women and Family Life* (New
York: Bobbs-Merrill Co., 1938).

measures which will assist it in realizing its highest potentialities. The concept of the family as a companionship embodies the ideals for the preservation of which we are waging this war—of democracy as the way of life, of the equality of men and women, and of personality as the highest human value. This new type of family is dynamic, adaptable, and creative—characteristics suited for survival and growth in a society in process of rapid social change.

BIBLIOGRAPHY

ANGELL, ROBERT C. *The Family Encounters the Depression.* New York, 1936.

BOSSARD, JAMES H. S. "War and the Family," *American Sociological Review*, VI (June, 1941), 330–44.

BUCK, PEARL, "Women and Victory," in *American Unity and Asia*, chap. ix. New York, 1942.

CUBER, JOHN F. "The College Youth Goes to War," *Marriage and Family Living*, Vol. V (February, 1943).

DE VINNEY, LELAND; OGBURN, WILLIAM; and VALENTINE, ALAN. *War and the Family.* A University of Chicago Round Table Transcript, No. 215, broadcast April 26, 1942.

DUVALL, EVELYN MILLIS. "Marriages in War Time," *Marriage and Family Living*, IV (November, 1942), 72–75.

GLUECK, ELEANOR T. "War Time Delinquency," *Journal of Criminal Law and Criminology*, XXXIII (July–August, 1942), 119–35.

GRUENBERG, SIDONIE M. (ed.). *The Family in a World at War.* New York, 1942.

OGBURN, WILLIAM F., and TIBBITTS, CLARK. "The Family and Its Functions," in *Recent Social Trends in the United States*, chap. xxii. New York, 1933.

PINNEY, JEAN B. "How Fares the Battle against Prostitution?" *Social Service Review*, XVI (June, 1942), 224–46.

RECKLESS, WALTER C. "Impact of War on Crime, Delinquency, and Prostitution," *American Journal of Sociology*, XLVIII (November, 1942), 378–86.

WALLER, WILLARD. *War and the Family.* New York, 1940.

THE AMERICAN TOWN

W. LLOYD WARNER

☼

THE discussion in this chapter is divided into two parts. In the first, some of the more general effects of the war on the town's social life are described; in the second and larger part, two significant aspects of the war's influence are studied. The first topic is confined to this one section. It is necessarily brief, since the other chapters of this book, in covering what is happening to the population, family life, economic organization, crime, and other important parts of American life, have supplied much of the basic knowledge about the war's impact on the town. The second part of this paper will continue through the two remaining sections and will deal with the effect the war is having on the institutions, unity, and symbolic life of the American town.

SOCIAL CHANGES IN THE TOWNS

The most casual survey supplies ample evidence that the effects of the present war are most varied and diverse as they are reflected in the life of American towns. The war's influence is very great in some towns and very little in others. It strengthens the social structure of some and greatly weakens the social systems of others. In some communities it appears to be introducing very little that is new, while in others the citizens have been compelled by force of circumstances to incorporate whole new experiences into their lives and into the social systems which control them. In some communities there has been no decided increase or decrease in the population, and the war has not changed the ordinary occupations of their people. Their citizens have made but minor adjustments in their daily lives; no basic changes have occurred in their institutions. For example, there are many small market towns servicing rural areas about them where the present round of events is substantially repeating what occurred last year and all previous years from the time the towns grew to early maturity. A few of their boys have been drafted, possibly the money crop is more remunerative, and it may be that the weekly paper has a few more war stories. Changes there are, but they are few and minor in their effect on the basic social system.

At the other extreme most drastic and spectacular changes have occurred. Small towns that formerly existed have disappeared entirely, and their former localities are occupied by industrial cities born since the war and fathered by it. Sleepy rural villages have been supplanted by huge industrial populations recruited from every corner of America. Towns of a few hundreds, traditionally quiet and well composed, have suddenly expanded into brawling young cities with no past and with only a problematical future. Market towns have become industrial areas. The wives and mothers of these towns have left their homes and joined the newcomers on the assembly line. The old people have gone back into industry to take jobs they must learn like the youngest boy working beside them. This boy and some of his friends have quit high school because they received tacit encouragement from their elders and the school authorities to go to work to help in the war effort. In some communities the whole system of control that formerly prevailed has ceased to function or has been superseded by outside authority. The influx of population has been so great that the schools can teach but a small portion of the children. The police force is inadequate. The usual recreational life has disappeared to be supplanted by the taxi dance, juke joint, beer hall, and gambling dive. Institutions such as the church and lodge have almost ceased to function. In some towns one can drive through miles of trailer camps and small houses pressed against each other, all recently assembled, where the inhabitants are living in squalid anonymity with, but not of, the thousands around them. They are an aggregate of individuals concentrated in one area, but they are not a community.

So far we have described the two extremes. Soon, however, those communities which have been little affected by the war will feel its full effects, and those which have been disorganized will in time develop habits of life which will conform to the ordinary pattern of American town life. The two extremes will tend to approximate the average. But the war is influencing the average town quite differently. Changes are taking place, the institutional life is being modified, new experiences are being felt by the people, and the townsmen are repeatedly modifying their behavior to adapt to new circumstances brought them by the events of the war. But these modifications are not causing social breakdown. The contrary is true. The war activities are strengthening the integration of many of our small communities. The people are being more systematically organized into groups where everyone is involved and in which there is an intense awareness of oneness. The towns' unity and feeling of autonomy are strengthened by competition in war activities with neighboring communities.

It is clear even now that the unifying experiences of the war will further remove symbolic differences and social divisions which now partly separate ethnic and religious organizations from the main stream of our cultural life. Unless our system of distribution changes radically, the chances of basic modification in our social groups seem small. However, if the belief in the virtues of the middle class is lost and if the incomes of such people are removed, the solid support that our present system receives from this "superior" class of the small towns will certainly be gone. If the war extends for a long period of time and we continue to suffer reverses, our present social economy and type of local and national political leadership will be distrusted, possibly eliminated, and a new type of personnel may fill the higher brackets of our society.

THE DEVELOPMENT OF EQUALITARIAN INSTITUTIONS

The thesis of this second section of the chapter is that wars modify (and only wars can) our social structure to create unique types of democratic institutions which express values which are very highly prized in American life. The second thesis, and the third part of this paper, asserts that war, and only war, creates a type of sacred symbol system which we are supposed to treasure as a democratic people and which strongly influences the whole life of the community and greatly contributes to the lasting unity of the group.

In proof of these theses I shall present evidence from studies made of the social and symbolic organizations of towns in New England, the South, and the Middle West. We must first briefly describe the social system of modern American towns to establish what is being influenced by the war in order to prepare ourselves for understanding how this war is contributing to our social and symbolic life. We must be content here with a composite picture.

The towns' traditions are ordinarily old American, of which their people are very proud. Yet only about half to three-fourths of the people are American of three or more generations. The others are French-Canadians, Poles, Italians, Jews, Irish, and Russians, who, while fast becoming American, still maintain social subsystems within the life of the town. These minority groups and the older Americans belong to a large number of churches, which are divided into basic faiths: Protestant, Roman Catholic, Jewish, and often Greek Orthodox.

There is a number of social levels, five or six in all, which unequally distribute the goods and labor of the economic system and the rights, privileges, duties, and in general the things wanted and not wanted which are available in varying quantities for the people of the community. The six class levels consist of an upper class divided into a top old-family stratum and a lower new-family one; upper- and lower-middle class; and two lower-class strata.

Obviously such communities with greatly differentiated economic, class, ethnic, and religious groupings have a highly complex social system. There are many partially autonomous subsystems within; and heterogeneity characterizes their life.

The associational institutions tend to cover a wider spread of social levels in their membership than do the families and cliques, but often they are used, and very frequently consciously, to emphasize class, ethnic, and religious differences. Our researches record nineteen types of associations based on combinations of members from the six classes in one community. Present studies now under way in other American areas reveal similar situations. They vary in composition from associations with only upper-class or those with only lower-class members to those which have representatives from all classes present. Less than 6 per cent of the several hundred associations include members from all classes. Of the remaining 94 per cent, approximately half have representatives from only three classes or less than three. Although the associations which include members from all levels of the community are surprisingly few, those which stress in action as well as in words such other principles of democracy as the equality of races, nationalities, and religions are even fewer. Only 5 per cent of the associations are composed of members from the four religious faiths—Protestant, Catholic, Jewish, and Greek Orthodox—and most of their members came from the lower ranks of the society. Only an infinitesimal number of associations is sufficiently large and democratic in action to include in their membership men or women from all class levels, all religious faiths, and most, if not all, ethnic groups. Their number could be easily counted on the fingers of one hand. This is the group of associations to which we will give our attention. Most prominent among them is the patriotic association. The American Legion is a typical example of the patriotic group.

Why should the American Legion, sometimes accused of being intolerant and hostile to the opinions of variant groups, occupy this democratic position? The answer lies in the social context in which it was created. The American Legion was born of the experiences of the soldiers of the last war. It is an effort to maintain the values experienced by those who participated in the war. The Legion is not a new type of association. The Grand Army of the Republic, the Sons of Union Veterans, and the Spanish War Veterans are products of earlier wars. The Sons of Union Veterans, a nonmilitary group, testifies to the fact that war experiences are not just those of soldiers but of everyone in the community. Furthermore, in functioning to maintain the values of a war experienced by very few of its members, it demonstrates that something more is involved than the formation of an organization of soldiers. To find the answer we must ask what happens to the people of our communities in time of war.

It is in time of war that the average American small-towner gets his deepest satisfactions as a member of his society. Despite the pessimistic events of the first year of the war of 1917–18, the people derived deep satisfaction from it, just as they do from the present struggle. It is a mistake to believe that the American people, particularly the small-towners, hate war to the extent that they derive no satisfaction from it. Verbally and superficially they disapprove of war, but at best this is only partly revealed in their deeper feelings. In simple terms, their observed behavior reveals that most of them are having more real satisfaction out of the present war, just as they did in the last war, than they have had in any other period of their lives. The various men's and women's organizations, instead of inventing things to do to keep busy, are now having to choose between activities which they know are most vital and significant to them and to others.

The small-towner today has a sense of significance about himself, about those around him, and about the events which are occurring, in a way that he has never felt before. The same was true in 1917–18. The young man who quit high school during the depression to lounge on the street corner and who was known to be of no consequence to himself or to anyone else in the community is now a seasoned veteran fighting somewhere in the South Pacific—a man obviously with the qualities of a hero (it is believed), willing to give up his life for his country, since he is in our military forces. He and everyone else are playing, and they know they are playing, a vital and significant role in our present crisis. Everyone is in it. There is a feeling of unconscious well-being (what we sometimes call euphoria) because everyone is doing something to help in the common desperate enterprise in a co-operative rather than in a private spirit. This feeling is often the unconscious equivalent of what people mean when they gather to celebrate and sing "Hail, hail, the gang's all here." It also has something of the deep significance that only enters into people's lives in moments of tragedy.

The strong belief that everyone must sacrifice to win the war has greatly strengthened people's sense of their significance. Everyone is giving up something for the common good —money, food, tires, scrap, automobiles, or blood for blood banks. All of it is contributed under the basic ideology of common sacrifice for the good of the country. These simple acts of giving by all individuals in the town, by all families, associations, schools, churches, and factories, are given strong additional emotional support by the common knowledge that some of the local young men are representing the town in the military forces of the country. It is known that some of them may be killed while serving their country. They are sacrificing their lives, it is believed, that their country may live. Therefore, all acts of individual giving to help win the war, no matter how small, are made socially significant and add to the strength of the social structure by being treated as sacrifices. The collective effect of these small renunciations, it is believed, is to lessen the number of those who must die on the altars of their country.

Another very strong integrative factor contributed by the war for strengthening the social structure of the small town and city is that petty internal antagonisms are drained out of the group on to the common enemy. The local antagonisms which customarily divide and separate people are largely suppressed. The feelings and psychic energies involved, normally expended in local feuds, are vented on the hated symbols of the enemy. The local ethnic groups, too frequently excluded from participation in community affairs, are given an honored place in the war effort, and the symbols of unity are stressed rather than the separating differences. The religious groups and the churches tend to emphasize the oneness of the common war effort rather than to allow their differing theologies and competitive financing to keep them in opposing groups. The strongest pressure to compose their differences is placed against management and labor. The small number of strikes is eloquent proof of the effectiveness of such pressure. A common hate of a common enemy, when organized in community activities to express this basic emotion, provides the most powerful mechanism to energize the lives of our towns and to strengthen our feelings of unity. Those who believe that the war's hatreds can bring only evil to our psychic life might well ponder the therapeutic and satisfying effects on the minds of people who are turning their once private hatreds into social ones and joining their townsmen and countrymen in the feeling of sharing this basic emotion in common symbols. Enemies as well as friends should be well chosen, for they must serve as objects for the expression of two emotions basic to man and his social system—hatred and love.

The American Legion and other patriotic organizations give form to our effort to capture the feelings of well-being when the society was most integrated and feelings of unity were most intense. The membership comes from every class, creed, and nationality, for the soldiers came from all of them.

After the present war we can expect a very powerful association of soldiers to be formed. It is possible that organizations of men who fought in the major areas of the world will incorporate as separate groups or as subsidiaries to the larger; and, if the women's military enlistments grow sufficiently numerous, they will form local chapters similar to the men's organizations.

We may expect a period in American history when these veterans' organizations will play a dominant and often a decisive role in the small towns and in our national life. If the war lasts several years, their degree of influence will increase accordingly.

The fact that these veterans do not include the civilians who participated in the war-feeling needs further explanation, since we need to know how the experiences of the ordinary civilian are later organized into the life of the community. To do this, we must turn to the next section of our discussion.

THE DEVELOPMENT OF EQUALITARIAN SYMBOLS WHICH HELP UNIFY CLASSES AND CREEDS

Each year various groups of people in our towns engage in literally thousands of significant rites, always symbolic, which give visible and audible form to the feelings and beliefs of the participants. These symbolic events may be very elaborate religious ceremonies or extremely simple secular ones.

Their religious ceremonies are one of the several forms of collective representations which Durkheim so brilliantly defines and interprets in his book, *The Elementary Forms of the Religious Life*. He said, "Religious representations are collective representations which express collective realities." Religious collective representations are symbol systems which are composed of beliefs and rites which relate men to sacred beings. Beliefs are "states of opinion and consist in representations"; rites are "determined modes of action" which are expressions of and refer to religious belief. They are *visible* signs (symbols) of the invisible belief.

The religious ceremonies, periodically held, function to impress on men their social nature and make them aware of something beyond themselves which they feel and believe to be sacred. This intense feeling of belonging to something larger and more powerful than themselves and of having part of this within them as part of them is first symbolized by the belief in sacred beings, which is given a visual symbol by use of symbolic designs which are the emblems of the sacred entities.

That which is beyond, yet part of, one is no more than the awareness on the part of individuals and the collectivity of individuals of their participation in a social group. *The religious symbols as well as the secular ones must express the nature of the social structure of the group of which they are a part and which they represent.* The beliefs in the gods and the symbolic rites which celebrate their divinity are no more than men collectively worshiping their own images—their own since they were made by themselves and fashioned from their experiences among themselves.

Studies of the social structure and symbolic life of many tribes from the major regions of the earth indicate that the sacred symbolic life reflects the social system and functions to maintain it. The evidence from these other societies permits the formulation of a hypothesis and gives us an expectancy of what we might find in the towns of America. If the principles of our symbolism conform to those already cited, we would suppose that our symbol system would express the realities of our social structure. It is clear from the earlier description of the American town's social structure that it is extremely complex. There is great social differentiation, which means that these great differences should be related to some kind of extreme differentiation in our sacred symbols. We should expect to find numerous kinds of semi-autonomous symbol systems and probably several varieties of each kind.

The integration and smooth functioning of the social life of a modern community are very difficult because of the heterogeneity of the parts. We should therefore expect conflicting parts to have conflicting symbols; we know it is necessary for the community to provide itself with symbol systems which function to integrate the people into total community activities and permit the interrelation of these segmenting symbols. A considerable degree of unity is necessary if we are to maintain the ordinary functions of the group.

Our communities are filled with churches, each claiming great authority and each with its separate sacred symbol system. Many of them are in conflict, and all of them in opposition. Many of our associations, such as the Masons, Odd Fellows, and the like, have sacred symbol systems which partly separate them from the whole community. The ethnic traditions contribute to the heterogeneity of symbolic life. The evidence is clear on symbolic differentiation and the conflict among these systems. Do we have sacred symbol systems which permit integration and collective action through their use by everyone in the community?

It is the thesis of this paper that the Memorial Day ceremonies and subsidiary rites such as those of Armistice Day of today, yesterday, and tomorrow are rituals which are a sacred symbol system which functions to integrate the whole community, with its conflicting symbols and its opposing, autonomous churches and associations. It is contended here that in the Memorial Day ceremonies the anxieties man has about death are confronted with a system of sacred beliefs about death which gives the individuals involved and the collectivity of individuals a feeling of well-being. Further, the feeling of triumph over death by collective action in the Memorial Day parade is made possible by re-creating the feeling of euphoria and the sense of group strength and individual strength in the group power, which is felt so intensely during the wars when the veterans' associations are created and when the feeling so necessary for the Memorial Day's symbol system is originally experienced.

MEMORIAL DAY CEREMONIES

We shall first examine the Memorial Day ceremony of an American town for evidence. The sacred symbolic behavior of Memorial Day, in which scores of the town's organizations are involved, is ordinarily divided into four periods. During the year separate rituals are held by many of the associations for their dead, and many of these activities are connected with later Memorial Day events. In the second phase, preparations are made during the last three or four weeks for the ceremony itself, and some of the associations perform public rituals. The third phase consists of the scores of rituals held in all the cemeteries, churches, and halls of the associations. These rituals consist of speeches and highly ceremonialized behavior. They last for two days and are climaxed by the fourth and last phase in which all the separate celebrants gather in the center of the business district on the afternoon of Memorial Day. The separate organizations, with their members in uniform or with fitting insignia, march through the town, visit the shrines and monuments of the hero dead, and, finally, enter the cemetery. Here dozens of ceremonies are held; most of them are highly symbolic and formalized. Let us examine the actual ritual behavior in these several phases of the ceremony.

The two or three weeks before the Memorial Day ceremonies are usually filled with elaborate preparations by each participating group. Meetings are held, and patriotic pronouncements are sent to the local paper by the various organizations which announce what part the organization is to play in the ceremony. Some of the associations have Memorial Day processions, memorial services are conducted by some of them, the schools have patriotic programs, and the cemeteries are cleaned and repaired. Graves are decorated by families and associations and new gravestones purchased and erected. The merchants put up flags before their establishments, and residents place flags above their houses.

All these events are recorded in the local paper, and most of them are discussed by the town. The preparation of public opinion for an awareness of the importance of Memorial Day and the rehearsal of what is expected from each section of the community are done fully and in great detail. The latent sentiments of each individual, each family, each church, school, and association for its own dead are thereby stimulated and related to the sentiments for the dead of the nation.

One of the important events observed in the preparatory phase in our community studied occurred several days before Memorial Day when the man who had been war mayor wrote an open letter to the commander of the American Legion. It was published in the local paper. He had a city-wide reputation for patriotism. He was an honorary member of the American Legion. The letter read: "Dear Commander: The approaching Poppy Day [when the Legion blanketed the town with solicitors] brings to my mind a visit to the war zone in

France on Memorial Day, 1925, reaching Belleau Wood at about 11 o'clock. On this sacred spot we left floral tributes in memory of our town's boys—Jonathan Dexter and John Smith, who here had made the supreme sacrifice, that the principle that 'might makes right' should not prevail."

Three days later the paper in a front-page editorial told its readers: "Next Saturday is the annual Poppy Day of the American Legion. Everybody should wear a poppy on Poppy Day. Think back to those terrible days when the red poppy on Flanders Field symbolized the blood of our boys slaughtered for democracy." The editor here explicitly states the symbolism involved.

Through the early preparatory period of the ceremony, through all its phases and in every rite, the emphasis in all communities is always on sacrifice—the sacrifice of the lives of the soldiers of the city willingly given for democracy and for their country. The theme is always that the gift of their lives was voluntary; that it was freely given and therefore above selfishness or thoughts of self-preservation; and, finally, that the "sacrifice on the altars of their country" was done for everyone. The red poppy became a separate symbol from Mc-Crae's poem, "In Flanders Fields." The poem expressed and symbolized the sentiments experienced by the soldiers and people of the country who went through the last war. The editor makes the poppy refer directly to the "blood of the boys slaughtered." In ritual language he then recites the names of some of the city's "sacrificed dead," and "the altars" (battles) where they were killed. "Remember Dexter and Smith killed at Belleau Wood," he says. "Remember O'Flaherty killed near Château-Thierry, Stulavitz killed in the Bois d'Ormont, Kelley killed at Côte de Chatillon, Jones near the Bois de Montrebeaux, Kilnikap in the St.-Mihiel offensive, and the other brave boys who died in camp or on stricken fields. Remember the living boys of the Legion on Saturday."

The names selected by the editor covered most of the ethnic and religious groups of the community. They included Polish, Russian, Irish, French-Canadian, and Yankee names. The use of such names in this context emphasized the fact that the voluntary sacrifice of a citizen's life was equalitarian. They covered the top, middle, and bottom of the several classes. The newspapers throughout the country are now printing [May, 1943] similar lists, and their editorials are stressing the equality of sacrifice by all classes and creeds.

The topic for the morning services of the churches on the Sunday before Memorial Day ordinarily is the meaning of Memorial Day to the town and to the people as Christians. All the churches participate. Because of space limitations, we shall quote from only a few sermons from one Memorial Day to show the main themes, but observations of Memorial Day behavior after this war began show no difference in the principal themes expressed before and after the present war started. Indeed, some of the words in both are almost interchangeable. The Rev. Hugh McKellar chose as his text "Be thou faithful until death." He said:

> Memorial Day is a day of sentiment and when it loses that it loses all its value. We are all conscious of the danger of losing that sentiment. What we need today is more sacrifice, for there can be no achievement without sacrifice. There are too many out today preaching selfishness. Sacrifice is necessary to a noble living. In the words of our Lord, "Whosoever shall save his life shall lose it and whosoever shall lose his life in My name shall save it." It is only those who sacrifice personal gain and will to power and personal ambition who ever accomplish anything for their nation. Those who expect to save the nation will not get wealth and power for themselves.
>
> Memorial Day is a religious day. It is a day when we get a vision of the unbreakable brotherhood and unity of spirit which exists and still exists, no matter what race or creed or color, in the country where all men have equal rights.

The minister of the Congregational church spoke with the voice of the Unknown Soldier to emphasize his message of sacrifice:

If the spirit of that Unknown Soldier should speak, what would be his message? What would be the message of a youth I knew myself who might be one of the unknown dead? I believe he would speak as follows: "It is well to remember us today, who gave our lives that democracy might live, we know something of sacrifice."

The two ministers in different language expressed the same theme of the sacrifice of the individual for national and democratic principles. One introduces divine sanction for this sacrificial belief and thereby succeeds in emphasizing the theme that the loss of an individual's life rewards him with life eternal. The other uses one of our greatest and most sacred symbols of democracy and the only very powerful one that came out of the last war—the Unknown Soldier. The American Unknown Soldier is Everyman of the mystery plays. He is the perfect symbol of equalitarianism.

There were many more Memorial Day sermons, most of which had this same theme. Many of them added the point that the Christian god had given his life for all. That afternoon during the same ceremony the cemeteries, memorial squares named for the town's dead, the lodge halls, and the churches had a large number of rituals. Among them was the "vacant chair." A row of chairs decorated with flags and wreaths, each with the name of a veteran who had died in the last year, was the center of this ceremony held in a church. Most of the institutions were represented in the ritual. We shall give only a small selection from the principal speech:

Now we come to pay tribute to these men whose chairs are vacant, not because they were eminent men, as many soldiers were not, but the tribute we pay is to their attachment to the great cause. We are living in the most magnificent country on the face of the globe, a country planted and fertilized by a Great Power, a power not political or economic but religious and educational, especially in the North. In the South they had settlers who were there in pursuit of gold, in search of El Dorado, but the North was settled by people seeking religious principles and education.

In a large city park, before a tablet filled with the names of war dead, one of our field workers shortly after the vacant-chair rite heard a speaker in the memorial ritual eulogize the two great symbols of American unity—Washington and Lincoln. The orator said:

No character except the Carpenter of Nazareth has ever been honored the way Washington and Lincoln have been in New England. Virtue, freedom from sin, and righteousness were qualities possessed by Washington and Lincoln, and in possessing these characteristics both were true Americans, and we would do well to emulate them. Let us first be true Americans. From these our friends beneath the sod we receive their message, "Carry on." Though your speaker will die, the fire and spark will carry on. Thou are not conqueror, death, and thy pale flag is not advancing.

In all the other services the same themes were used in the speeches, most of which were in ritualized, oratorical language, or expressed in the ceremonials themselves. Washington, the father of his country, first in war and peace, had devoted his life not to himself but to his country. Lincoln had given his own life, sacrificed on the altar of his country. Most of the speeches implied or explicitly stated that divine guidance was involved and that these mundane affairs had supernatural implication. They stated that the revered dead had given the last ounce of devotion in following the ideals of Washington and Lincoln and the Unknown Soldier and declared these same principles must guide us, the living.

The beliefs and values of which they spoke referred to a world beyond the natural. Their references were to the supernatural.

On Memorial Day morning the separate rituals, publicly performed, continued. The parade formed in the early afternoon in the business district. Hundreds of people gathered to watch the various uniformed groups march in the parade. They were dressed in their best. Crowds collected along the whole route. The cemeteries, carefully prepared for the event, and the graves of kindred covered with flowers and flags and wreaths looked almost gay.

The parade marched through the town to the cemeteries. The various organizations spread throughout the several parts of the graveyards, and rites were performed. In the Greek quarter ceremonies were held; others were performed in the Polish and Russian sections; the Boy Scouts held a memorial rite for their departed; the Sons and Daughters of Union Veterans went through a ritual, as did the other men's and women's organizations. All this was part of the parade in which everyone from all parts of the community could and did participate.

Near the end of the day all the men's and women's organizations assembled about the roped-off grave of General Fredericks. The Legion band played. A minister uttered a prayer. The ceremonial speaker said:

We meet to honor those who fought, but in so doing we honor ourselves. From them we learn a lesson of sacrifice and devotion and of accountability to God and honor. We have an inspiration for the future today—our character is strengthened—this day speaks of a better and greater devotion to our country and to all that our flag represents.

After the several ceremonies in the Elm Hill Cemetery, the parade re-formed and started the march back to town, where it broke up. The firing squad of the American Legion fired three salutes, and a drummer blew taps outside the cemetery's front entrance as they departed. This, they said, was a "general salute for all the dead in the cemetery."

Here we see people who are Protestant, Catholic, Jewish, and Greek Orthodox involved in a common ritual in a graveyard with their common dead. Their sense of autonomy was present and expressed in the separate ceremonies, but the parade and unity of doing everything at one time emphasized the oneness of the total group. Each ritual also stressed the fact that the war was an experience where everyone sacrificed and some died, not as members of a separate group, but as citizens of a whole community.

HOW SUCH CEREMONIES FUNCTION IN THE COMMUNITY

It is the thesis of this chapter that the Memorial Day rites of American towns are a modern cult of the dead and conform to Durkheim's definition of sacred collective representations. They are a cult because they consist of a system of sacred beliefs and dramatic rituals held by a group of people who, when they congregate, represent the whole community. They are sacred because they ritually relate the living to sacred things. They are a cult because the members have not been formally organized into an institutionalized church with a defined theology but depend on informal organization to order their sacred activities. They are called a cult here because this term most accurately places them in a class of social phenomena clearly identified in the sacred behavior of non-European societies.

The cult system of sacred belief conceptualizes in organized form sentiments common to everyone in the community about death. These sentiments are composed of fears of death which conflict with the social reassurances our culture provides us to combat such anxieties. These assurances, usually acquired in childhood and thereby carrying some of the authority of the adults who provided them, are a composite of theology and folk belief. The deep anxieties to which we refer include anticipation of our deaths, of the deaths or possible deaths of loved ones, and, less powerfully, of the deaths or possible deaths of those we know and of men in general.

Each man's church provides him and those of his faith with a set of beliefs and a mode of action to face these problems, but his church and those of other men do not equip him with a common set of social beliefs and rituals which permit him to unite with all his fellows to confront this common and most feared of all his enemies. The Memorial Day rite and other subsidiary rituals connected with it form a cult which partially satisfies this need for common action on a common problem. It dramatically expresses the sentiments of unity of all the living among themselves, of all the living to all the dead, and of all the living and dead as a group to the gods. The gods—Catholic, Protestant, and Jewish—lose their sectarian definitions, limitations, and foreignness among themselves and become objects of worship for the whole group and the protectors of everyone.

The unifying and integrating symbols of this cult are the dead. The graves of the dead are the most powerful of the visible emblems which unify all the activities of the separate groups of the community. The cemetery and its graves become the objects of sacred rituals which permit opposing organizations, often in conflict, to subordinate their ordinary opposition and to co-operate in collectively expressing the larger unity of the total community through the use of common rites for their collective dead. The rites show extraordinary respect for all the dead, but they pay particular honor to those who were killed in battle "fighting for their country." The death of a soldier in battle is believed to be a "voluntary sacrifice" by him on the altar of his country. To be understood, this belief in the sacrifice of a man's life for his country must be judged first with our general scientific knowledge on the nature of all forms of sacrifice. It then must be subjected to the principles which explain human sacrifice whenever and wherever found. More particularly, this belief must be examined with the realization that these sacrifices occur in a society whose deity was a man who sacrificed his life for all men.

The principle of the gift is involved. In simple terms, when something valuable is given, an equally valuable thing must be returned. The speaker who quoted Scripture in his Memorial Day speech, "Whosoever shall save his life shall lose it and whosoever shall lose his life in My name shall save it," almost explicitly stated the feelings and principles involved. Finally, and most particularly, the analysis we make of the belief in "the sacrifice of American citizens killed in battle" is that it is done for their country and its people and their collective moral principles.

With these thoughts in mind, let us turn our attention again to the ceremony. The ceremony consists of a series of separate rituals performed by autonomous groups which culminate in a procession *of all of them as one group* to the consecrated area set aside by the living for their dead. In such a place the dead are classed as individuals, for their graves are separate; as members of separate social situations, for they are found in family plots and formal ritual respect is paid them by church and association; and as a collectivity, since they are thought of as "our dead" in most of the ceremonies. The fences surrounding the cemetery place all the dead together and separate all the living from them.

The Memorial Day rite is a cult of the dead, but not just of the dead as such, since by symbolically elaborating sacrifice of human life for the country through, or identifying it with, the Christian church's sacred sacrifice of their god, the deaths of such men also become powerful sacred symbols which organize, direct, and constantly revive the collective ideals of the community and the nation. In brief, this sacrificial cult is a collective representation which tends to make sacred our ideas and feelings about the state and our subordinate and dependent status as citizens.

Just as the totemic symbol system of the Australians represents the idealized clan, and the African ancestral worship symbolizes the family and state, so the Memorial Day rites symbolize and express the sentiments the people have for the total community and the state. But, in so doing, the separate values and ideas of various parts of the community are also portrayed. The ideas and values of several religions, ethnic groups, classes, associations, and other groupings are symbolically expressed and their place within the social structure of the community clearly indicated.

We can predict that the organizations developing from this war will greatly strengthen the present set of patriotic societies and conscious and unconscious feelings expressed in the sacred ideology. If the present war continues for several years and we win, the feelings will be more intense than those which developed during the shorter period of the last war, and the beliefs and ceremonies will be accordingly more powerful. The generation which fought the last war is still active and powerful in the community. They may try to organize the younger generation of fighters with their own units, but, whatever happens to the organized form, the sacred beliefs and practices which I have called a modern cult of the dead will grow and exercise a more powerful effect on the community. This will happen because the present war is rapidly destroying many social barriers that separate people. The developing feelings of unity are going to be expressed in more powerful collective representations than we now possess.

BIBLIOGRAPHY

DAVIS, ALLISON, and GARDNER, BURLEIGH B. and MARY. *Deep South*. Chicago, 1941.

DOLLARD, JOHN. *Caste and Class in a Southern Town*. New Haven, 1937.

DURKHEIM, EMILE. *The Elementary Forms of the Religious Life*. New York, 1915.

JONES, A. W. *Life, Liberty and Property*. New York, 1941.

LYND, R. A. and H. M. *Middletown: A Study in Contemporary American Culture*. New York, 1929.

――――. *Middletown: A Study in Cultural Conflict*. New York, 1937.

MILLER, NEAL, and DOLLARD, JOHN. *Social Learning and Imitation*. New Haven, 1941.

WARNER, W. L., and LUNT, P. S. (eds.). *The Social Life of a Modern Community*. "Yankee City Series." New Haven, 1941.

――――. *The Status System of a Modern Community*. "Yankee City Series." New Haven, 1942.

THE URBAN COMMUNITY

LOUIS WIRTH

THE American cities, which are known throughout the world for their remarkably rapid and disorderly growth, have probably never undergone more profound and rapid changes than those precipitated by the war. To understand these changes, it is necessary to view cities in the light of the long-run trends, the depression period preceding the defense and war effort, and the wartime transformations themselves.

URBAN TRENDS

The most marked change of the past few decades in reference to cities is the phenomenal decline in their rate of growth.[1] Our urban population in the decade 1930–40 grew by only 7.9 per cent—the smallest percentage increase in our entire national history. For the first time some of our largest cities failed to show an increase in numbers, and 27 of our 93 cities with 100,000 and more population actually lost residents. The mushroom growth of cities which characterized the nineteenth and early twentieth centuries seems to have come to an end. Only in the South, the Southwest, and the Pacific area has the pace of urban growth failed to slacken to a point of alarm to the speculative-minded who saw in the limitless growth of cities the refutation of the claim that America had reached her frontiers.

The changing pattern of urban growth during the past few

[1] Louis Wirth, "Urban Communities," *American Journal of Sociology*, XLVII (May, 1942), 829–40.

decades has been almost as significant as the declining rate of growth itself. The concentration of industry and business in the larger urban centers has been accompanied by the centrifugal movement of residents seeking to escape into more favorable places in which to live. This desire to be free from the disadvantages, the costs, the restrictions, and the responsibilities of central urban location has also been shared by industries, which have increasingly abandoned the old industrial sites within the cities in favor of undeveloped suburban areas. The fact that nearly one out of six Americans in 1940 was a suburbanite and that there was one suburban dweller for every two inhabitants of a metropolitan city has profound implications for local government, real estate values, taxation, and city planning.

The serious problems created for the cities by the flight of industry and residents into the suburban fringe are complicated by the outward movement of residential and business districts within the cities themselves. The depopulation of the cores of cities has been accompanied by blight and physical decay, by declining revenue in the face of increasing costs, and by civic irresponsibility and the increasing impotence of cities to deal with their problems.[2]

THE IMPACT OF THE DEPRESSION

The onset of the depression of the thirties, following in the wake of unprecedented expansion and prosperity, accentuated the pace of the urban decline already apparent by the turn of this century.[3] Nation-wide mass unemployment, particularly in the urban centers, the wiping-out of savings, the undermining of the credit of urban governments, and the enormously

[2] Louis Wirth, "The Metropolitan Region as a Planning Unit," in *National Conference on Planning: Proceedings of the Conference Held at Indianapolis, Indiana, May 25–27, 1942* (Chicago, 1942).

[3] Homer Hoyt, "The Structure of American Cities in the Post-war Era," *American Journal of Sociology*, XLVIII (January, 1943), 475–81.

increased responsibilities of urban communities for destitute citizens left many cities prostrate. On the other hand, the depression, among other things, exploded the ancient myth of local self-sufficiency. Neither the cities nor the states found themselves able, unaided, to insure the minimum standard of subsistence for their people and the orderly functions of their institutions and public services.

The depression, like perhaps no other period in our history since the days of the frontier, also rekindled a new sense of collective responsibility for the welfare of all the citizenry through the proliferation of self-help institutions and organizations and through the emergence of a governmental policy of relief and public works designed to maintain at least a semblance of the American standard of living and to salvage something in the way of permanent gains out of the wreckage of national disaster. Despite the fact that large-scale public works and work-relief projects had to be improvised, and in the face of the resistance to deficit spending, most of our cities were able to take some measures to halt further physical and social disintegration and even gain some permanent improvements through the governmental aid that came during the decade of the depression.[4]

THE PERIOD OF DEFENSE AND WAR MOBILIZATION

Scarcely had the urban communities of America recoiled from the economic paralysis of the thirties when they were struck by the defense boom and the call for war mobilization. An army of unemployed estimated at over eight million at the beginning of 1940 was reduced to less than half that size by the end of 1941, and, as additional men were called into the armed forces and into the war industries, a labor surplus was soon

[4] E. W. Burgess, "A Close-up of Modern Main Street," in Florence C. Bingham (ed.), *Community Life in a Democracy* (Chicago: National Congress of Parents and Teachers, 1942), chap. i; Louis Wirth, "The New Birth of Community Consciousness," *ibid.*, chap. ii.

turned into a labor shortage for the country as a whole, though not for all regions and urban communities. As the size of the armed forces and the requirements of war industries mounted, the burdens on relief rolls and on work-relief projects shrank precipitately, leading to a clamor for the abandonment of the agencies administering these services.

Some of the advances we have made during the years of economic adversity stood us in good stead when war came upon us and are on the way to becoming permanent gains. Among them are our recognition of the need for equalization of educational opportunity, the protection of childhood and youth, the maintenance of minimum standards of housing, health, and welfare for all of our people, public assurance of the security of small savings, of minimum wages, of maximum hours, and the right to bargain collectively. If many of our communities, rural as well as urban, throughout the land can point to their modern schools, libraries, recreational and cultural facilities, health and welfare institutions, and many other physical improvements not visible to the naked eye, it is only because during the period of depression and at least part of the way into the period of war mobilization we carried out a nation-wide program of relief and reconstruction which in many respects left the communities of the nation in a more wholesome state than it found them. As a result, our American cities faced the call to war with greater unity, health, skills, and productive power, and understanding of what they are fighting for and against, than could possibly have been true otherwise. The ravages of the depression are still visible, of course, at least to the expert; but the scars on our cities and their people are less marked than they would have been without the resolute national policies that were taken, often against bitter opposition, and they are rapidly being obscured by the consequences of feverish war activity which are especially apparent in our urban centers.

WARTIME CHANGES

While no part of the nation has escaped the impact of war, the effect has by no means been the same in the different urban communities. The principal factor accounting for the differential effect of the war upon urban communities is the degree to which the different urban communities have been utilized in war production. This, in turn, has been significantly influenced by the location policies of the Plant Site Board of the War Production Board and by our form of contract-letting. There is a tendency in the distribution of contracts to produce further concentration of industries and people into a limited number of urban areas in many of which inadequate housing and community facilities already prevail.[5]

Approximately three-fourths of the new war plants are located within the metropolitan areas of cities with a population of over 100,000. The distribution of war industries is also creating a number of new settlements, many of which are acquiring the stature of imposing urban communities within a few weeks or months, thus telescoping the growing pains of urbanization into a short time span. In the same process those established urban communities which were by-passed in the war contract-letting are losing population through out-migration and are in some instances being reduced to ghost towns. With declining revenues and increasing costs per capita, these municipalities are experiencing hardships which, while not so dramatic as those of the boom towns, are nevertheless severe.

The population shifts produced by the industrial conversion and expansion incident to the defense, lend-lease, and war production programs are so recent and in such a state of flux that

[5] U.S. Congress, House of Representatives, *National Defense Migration: Fifth Interim Report of the Select Committee Investigating National Defense Migration* (77th Cong., 2d sess.; pursuant to H.R. 113, "Recommendations on the Mobilization of Manpower for the All-Out War Effort" [Washington: Government Printing Office, 1942]); cf. also Robert K. Lamb, "Mobilization of Human Resources," *American Journal of Sociology*, XLVIII (November, 1942), 323–30.

current and authentic information about them is scarce. The findings of the Tolan Committee, which investigated these migrations, give some indication of the scope and nature of these changes, as do the figures based on the number of registrations for sugar ration cards as of May, 1942.[6]

According to the Bureau of the Census, which analyzed the sugar ration registration, 88 of 137 metropolitan counties or groups of counties showed a gain between April 1, 1940, and May 1, 1942, while 43 showed a decline and 6 showed no appreciable change. In this brief period the gaining metropolitan counties increased by 2.6 million, or by 6.8 per cent of their 1940 civilian population. The greatest gain was in the southern urban areas and the greatest loss in the Northeast. In all except the southern metropolitan areas, the large metropolitan counties grew more rapidly than the small. Among the greatest gainers were the metropolitan counties of which the cities of Detroit, Washington, Chicago, Los Angeles, Norfolk–Portsmouth–Newport News, St. Louis, San Diego, San Francisco–Oakland are the metropolitan centers. The largest loss, amounting to 365,000, occurred in the New York–northeastern New Jersey metropolitan counties. On the whole it appears that the older settled sections of the country were bypassed by the war boom in favor of the newer sections.[7]

It is, of course, difficult to say, as long as our post-war industrial location policy is unsettled, whether these gains and losses will be permanent. It may be assumed, however, that those metropolitan areas which were expanding in the pre-war period have a better chance of retaining their wartime gains after the war than those that were declining. It is not out of

[6] U.S. Bureau of the Census, *Census of Population*, *Series P*-3 (Washington: Government Printing Office, 1942).

[7] Philip M. Hauser, "Population Shifts and Income Changes," an address delivered at the Wartime Marketing Conference of the American Management Association, January 15, 1943, at the Drake Hotel, Chicago.

the question, however, that certain metropolitan areas which have acquired war industries representing new technological developments usable for peacetime production may retain their gains or even enjoy a post-war growth in the face of pre-war decline. The war itself and the changed world organization that may follow it, together with the new forms of transportation and the altered international economic relations that seem likely to emerge, carry with them the potentiality of shifting the industrial and commercial base of many urban communities and consequently their relative position of dominance.

One of the most direct repercussions of the war upon our cities is the serious curtailment of maintenance work and the virtual cessation of all physical improvements involving critical materials and labor. This is in many cases delaying or preventing cities from reaping the benefits of anticipated and partially completed public facilities and is creating a backlog of public works for the period when construction can be resumed. Meanwhile, intensified wear-and-tear combined with accelerated obsolescence due to technological progress may be expected to increase the list of necessary and desirable rehabilitation and reconstruction measures to be undertaken by our cities after the war.[8]

The acute housing shortage created by the wholesale influx of war workers and the additional persons required to service them has been alleviated to some degree in a number of communities by the conversion of large apartments and single-family residences into smaller units accommodating several families. In some seriously overcrowded areas the Homes Registration Offices have attempted to relieve the housing shortage by the placement of newcomers as renters with established families. Unfortunately, the crowding and doubling-up result-

[8] American Society of Planning Officials, "Municipal Reserves for Post-war Public Works," *News Letter*, VIII (September, 1942), 1.

ing from these expedients usually fall most heavily upon the lower-income families, whose living quarters are more likely to be within easy access of the industrial areas than the less congested upper-income residential areas.

The tremendous expansion of war production has attracted to the urban industrial centers large numbers of in-migrants whose needs for housing and community services have created unanticipated demands upon cities. These demands frequently have had to go unmet because of lack of financial resources or restrictions on construction. Federal aid has been used extensively to meet the most essential needs of rapidly growing war areas but in many cases has had to be supplemented by local effort, often of an inadequate and improvised sort. Aside from war housing, the chief needs have been for water and sewage facilities, public utilities, education, health, fire protection and police services, recreation and day care for young children of working mothers.[9]

Trailer camps, tent colonies, and makeshift housing arrangements, coupled with planless and uncontrolled peripheral and suburban real estate developments adjacent to war plants, have complicated enormously the task of rendering adequate community services in urban areas. The contagious effect upon the city and its people of these new and amorphous settlements, frequently lying beyond the range of urban control, should not be underestimated. Not the least of the cities' concern is the fate of these boom areas when war production ceases. Considering the housing shortage that will exist when the war ends, it is unlikely that these temporary settlements will promptly be dismantled, despite the fact that they will constitute a serious menace to their inhabitants and their urban neighbors alike. Although they will constitute slums and will stand in the way of orderly and planful development

---

[9] U.S. Congress, *op. cit.*, and Lamb, *op. cit.*

of the urban areas, they may be allowed to linger on and perpetuate and spread their blight.

As the supply of civilian goods declines and the manpower problem becomes more acute, we may expect a continuous decline in the number and volume of business of retail establishments and small businesses. The number of vacancies in commercial real estate holdings is increasing, and in the absence of conversion to other uses property values may decline. The assessed value of real property in our larger cities has already shown this decline even in boom areas, especially in and near the cores of cities.

With the federal government absorbing a larger proportion of the available tax revenues, and with the abrupt decline of such typical state and local tax income as that derived from gasoline and vehicle taxes, respectively, the total public revenue of the cities may be expected to decline. The serious situation thus created is temporarily obscured if not mitigated by the fact that expenditures for physical improvements not entitled to high priorities have to be postponed, thus leaving artificial surpluses in the treasury. On the other hand, the cities, particularly those significantly affected by new war industries and in-migration, have been called upon to render greatly increased public services and not infrequently have had to pay more for them in order not to lose their employees to war industries paying wages and salaries more nearly commensurate with the rising cost of living.

The magnitude and suddenness of the in-migration of war workers into urban areas have not only taxed the service facilities of many cities heavily and wrenched their social structure out of shape but have in some instances aroused the antagonism of the established residents whose wishes in the nature of the case could not be consulted. Having had a flood of strangers thrust upon them, the medium-sized and smaller communities especially have occasionally been virtually cleft into two mutually hostile camps. The tensions between the old and the new residents have at times been aggravated by the fact that the new war industries are in the hands of management imported from the outside. The resentment against the newcomers is accentuated by the fact that they represent a heterogeneous group many of whom come from economically depressed regions or have been recruited from widely dispersed rural areas and have difficulties in making rapid adjustments to urban industrial ways of life. The relatively large proportion of unattached individuals among the in-migrants who are being uprooted from their home communities creates problems of vice and social disorganization which are difficult to control in a boom atmosphere and which arouse understandable anxieties among the indigenous families whose accustomed life is being dislocated. The fear that residential neighborhoods will deteriorate, that real estate values will decline, and that the boom will be only short-lived and will terminate suddenly and disastrously, leaving high taxation, debts, and devastation in its wake, accounts for much of the resistance and hostility to the wartime influx. The further fact that price control and particularly rent control prevent the old settlers from profiting greatly by the boom is not a negligible factor in generating this xenophobia.

Whatever the temporary friction between the old and new settlers of our cities may be, by attracting to urban jobs a welter of peoples from widely scattered areas, the war is accelerating the trek to the city and perhaps irreversibly urbanizing a large section of our rural peoples. The need for agricultural workers is just emerging as a grave national problem and may for at least a season or more produce a reflux of urbanites to the country. Although there appears no prospect that the emergency recruitment of urban young people and other potential farm laborers for agricultural work will find a substantial proportion of them remaining on the farms long after the war, these two-way interchanges of populations may do something toward minimizing the present differences between urban and rural ways of life.

Labor shortages have drawn many women, older persons, and young people who might otherwise have continued their schooling into employment. Combined with the higher wage scales and overtime pay, the increase in the proportion of the employed population, which by the end of 1943 is estimated to reach about fifty-five million, has raised the individual and family money income of the urban families to a prosperity level. This increased money income has not, however, resulted in correspondingly higher standards of living, because of price increases, heavier taxation, the stimulation given war savings, and the scarcity of consumer goods. On the other hand, rationing and price controls have to a large degree assured the more equitable distribution of the available commodities, with the result that the adverse effects of war economy, instead of accentuating the stratification along income lines, are tending toward greater democratization. The extreme contrasts between riches and poverty for which the cities have been noted are thus being minimized. It should be noted, however, that the urban population, because of its dependence on a money economy, is likely to feel the privations of war more seriously than the rural population, who retain some of the benefits of self-sufficiency, especially in respect to food.

Perhaps no single aspect of city life is as visibly different from the pre-war period as the marked reduction in private automobiles on the streets and in the parking lots. Tire and gasoline rationing has tremendously increased the traffic on the mass-transportation systems. To relieve these heavy loads during the rush hours, the suggestion of the Office of Defense Transportation, that work and school hours be staggered, has been heeded in many cities. Automobile riding pools, in which several individuals share cars with their neighbors and fellow-workers, have found virtually nation-wide acceptance. Not a few upper-income and white-collar suburbanites, because of both home-heating and transportation difficulties, have re-established residence in or near the centers of the city closer to their offices and places of work. The same factors, together with the prohibition of pleasure riding, may be presumed to have stimulated the cultivation of domestic and neighborly amusements, social relations, and forms of recreation. They have also adversely affected the use of the supermarkets and shopping and amusement centers beyond the limits of the immediate neighborhood.

Whereas the first World War gave a great and in many respects a lasting impetus to the community organization movement, World War II by virtue of its character as a total war is giving a rebirth to the social organization of our communities, especially our urban communities. The Civilian Defense organization and activities are in many communities welding nigh-dwellers into neighbors. The protective activities, such as civilian air-raid defense measures, which among other things have dimmed the bright lights on our Broadways and Main Streets in the coastal cities, and the fire prevention activities, while more spectacular than the rest, have not been the most significant except for those cities where the air-raid danger may still exist. The organization in our cities on a building, block, or zone basis of the formerly anonymous residents into salvage, bond sales, health, welfare, and educational units, however, has generated a new sense of social solidarity and community consciousness which has in many cases been strong enough to bridge economic, racial, religious, and ethnic barriers. The important role of such citizen organizations as draft boards and rationing boards in the assumption of essential responsibilities for the war effort is bringing to light a potential new basis for urban community living. New realms of co-operative action are emerging on many fronts.

Even in our giant cities many people who formerly were strangers to one another though living in adjoining apartments in the same building are for the first time making one another's acquaintance. The crisis of war is bringing to many people a new awareness of the community problems and of community resources to which they have hitherto been blind. Many communities have discovered a new meaning of the democratic spirit which their traditional political, religious, and social institutions have in the past failed to reveal. They have discovered the vast possibilities of and the satisfaction to be derived from citizen participation in local affairs. If we are able to salvage even a part of the war-born capacity for concerted community action for the peace to come, the cities may thereby find the strength and the means whereby to deal with some of their most serious problems which have hitherto defied solution.

DEMOBILIZATION

The longer the war lasts, the more profoundly will the structure of our urban communities be altered. That the cities of America were unprepared for war is clear from the unanticipated dislocations to which they were subjected when it struck. Hence many of the measures taken to readjust life to the tempo of war had to be improvised. They were often costly, clumsy, and inadequate. If we should be found as unprepared for demobilization day as we were for mobilization day, the consequences for urban communities and for the nation might be disastrous.

Fortunately, many of our urban communities, through their governments and organized civic bodies, are already busily at work considering the problems they will face when the armistice comes and the best ways of meeting them. They know that, when the war industries cease operations and when the armed forces return, they will confront a large-scale problem of re-employment in civilian pursuits. Factories will have to be reconverted; workers will have to be retrained and relocated; many of them, including some women, the aged, and the young, will wish to and probably should leave the labor market. The prompt revival of peacetime industry and commerce, upon which the survival and prosperity of cities depend, will, of course, be largely the task of private enterprise. Government policies as regards the cancellation of war contracts, the demobilization, compensation, and re-education of the armed forces, the disposal of war plants, foreign trade, taxation, and the control over scarce materials can, however, exert a decisive influence. Our social security system, built up during the depression, inadequate as it is, and the accumulated savings of the working population will do something to cushion the shock of the transition. Another important and necessary step will be the preparation now of plans for deferred public works to make good our past deficiencies, the obsolescence accentuated by war, the cessation and deferment of public improvements during the war, and the realization of objectives and possibilities that have emerged as a result of our new technology, of our new conception of a good community, and of the recognition of our huge productive capacity. The reserves in our state and local public treasuries will be of inestimable value in planning and initiating these public works.

In the struggle for survival many of our cities may be expected to make desperate attempts to hold on to the industrial gains they have made during the war and to resist the large-scale reshuffling of plants and opportunities for employment which industries and the nation may find necessary in the interests of an efficient economy. Fortunately, most of the new powder, explosives, and shell-loading plants, which are probably least adaptable to conversion, are located outside the metropolitan areas. Their workers may, at least in part, be reabsorbed by agriculture, from which they came. Those workers in the cities, however, who were recruited from other areas for war work may be the object of community hostility and discrimination, thus giving rise to tensions which are particularly dangerous in a shrinking economy. A nation-wide system of unemployment benefit payments irrespective of residence may be necessary to alleviate these antagonisms and relieve distress.

It would be a mistake, however, in the period of demobilization to plan merely for the return of the status quo and for the relief of the most severe consequences of unemployment. The American cities have an unprecedented opportunity not only to make up for their defects of the past but also to build for a better future.

POST-WAR URBAN RECONSTRUCTION

The urban America of tomorrow is in the making today. As an English observer has remarked about his country:

The longer the war lasts, the more will the problem of reconstruction be simply factual. The essential thing to observe is that there has begun to be a new order now. War is a forced experiment in government and social organization. The choice at the end of war will largely be one of how much of this new system is to be kept, partly on its then merits, because it is there, partly because we are likely to continue to require what may be called a defense economy. . . . . The way in which war contributes to a new order . . . . is chiefly due to the experience of war and the conditions it itself creates.[10]

Although we cannot predict the length of the war, we can become cognizant of the fact that the longer the war lasts the more will the changes produced by the war affect what we shall be able to do when the war is over.

The rebuilding of urban America, however, does not start

[10] D. H. MacGregor, "Actual War Influences in Reconstruction," *Agenda*, I (January, 1942), 3–12.

with a clean slate. In the post-war period we shall not have the opportunity to build new cities as we did a century ago. But we shall be forced, and have an unprecedented opportunity, to reconstruct the old cities, many of which have been created in response to conditions which have ceased to exist. Much as we might like to forget the old and start anew, our plans for reconstruction must therefore for some time to come be largely directed toward remedying the obvious defects which the experiences of history, and particularly the war, have revealed. If we recognize that the distortions of war have been superimposed upon a situation which was far from satisfactory at the beginning, we shall better appreciate the nature of the task confronting us.

With a technology born of wartime necessity and experience, new industrial products and processes will come to the fore. Entire new industries may actually come into being and old industries be revolutionized. We have made only the barest beginning in designing new modes of dwelling and new methods for prefabricating and building houses. If we can create a modern housing industry, as we have an automobile industry, to supply a mass market amounting to from one to one and a half million units a year for a period of at least ten years, we shall not only be contributing to much-needed employment opportunities but we shall have a means for changing the physical complexion of our cities. It is already apparent that the great strides in aviation will affect the internal structure of cities and the national urban pattern. The newer city plans now in the making are taking cognizance of the opportunities and needs created by the expected development and expansion of air passenger and freight traffic and the perfection of the helicopter. The strain to which our railroad and local mass transport system has been subjected during the war, together with the possible development of aviation and the redesign of the passenger automobile, appears to call for a reintegration of our entire transportation system and the reconstruction of existing and the creation of new facilities, including airports, terminals, parking spaces, and street and highway systems.

Just as the airplane has been interpreted by some to spell a revolutionary change in the relationship between hitherto distant places as a result of which some cities will lose their functions as concentration and intersection points in the movement of goods, people, and ideas, so the development of huge hydroelectric power projects, which will spread electric energy over wide and thus far undeveloped areas, has been interpreted as involving a shift to new urban centers of gravity. The modern industrial plants on the peripheries of our cities may be expected to be preferred sites for post-war industries over the older and relatively obsolescent plants near the centers of cities. This may accelerate the further deaggregation of urban areas and accentuate the blight of the urban cores. Instead of living in the suburbs and commuting to the cities to work, it may become normal for a substantial part of the working population, pending the development of residential communities near the peripheral industries, to live in the city and to commute to the suburbs to work.

To reconstruct the city in a manner to conserve existing values and to take advantage of newly won opportunities require planning now. Cities must be given much-needed powers to acquire land for public purposes and to control construction and transportation. They will be called upon to render greatly enlarged public services in health, welfare, education, recreation, and cultural opportunities. They will need a closer relationship to the states and to the federal government, and they will need increased powers to finance local services. The new urban area that is coming into being will probably be less densely aggregated, but it will have a wider areal scope extending far beyond its present municipal boundaries. A new unit of government—the metropolitan region—is emerging and beckoning for official recognition.

The demonstration of the existence of hitherto unutilized productive resources that has taken place during the war has given to the American people a vision of a greatly enlarged horizon of the possible. The rekindled hope for a fuller realization of the substance of democracy in the post-war period, based upon the prospects of a satisfactory level of employment, a wider distribution of physical comforts, education, recreation, health, and cultural opportunity, widens the chasm between the actual conditions of life as we find them among the masses of men in our cities and the aspirations for a better life to which the American people are giving voice. The kind of cities that the American people want will be significantly influenced by the degree to which their ideals of freedom and security and their conception of the satisfactions worth striving for can be shown to be realizable in the foreseeable future and by the degree in which science, planning, and statesmanship can show the way to translate these ideals into realities.

If the cities of the future, which are being molded in the caldron of war, will take advantage of the lessons the war has taught and will translate our national ideals into local gains for their people, the country as a whole will be the healthier and the richer for it, for whatever gains the cities might make will ultimately be reflected upon the rural areas as well.

BIBLIOGRAPHY

An Appraisal Technique for Urban Problem Areas as a Basis for Housing Policy of Local Governments: Illustrative Results from Three Test Surveys. American Public Health Association, Committee on the Hygiene of Housing, Reprint No. 2359. 1942.

BINGHAM, FLORENCE C. (ed.). *Community Life in a Democracy.* Chicago, 1942.

CHASE, STUART. *Goals for America: A Budget of Our Needs and Resources*. New York, 1942.

———. *The Road We Are Traveling: 1914–42*. New York, 1942.

COLEAN, MILES J. *The Role of the Housebuilding Industry*. Washington, D.C., 1942.

FEDERAL HOUSING ADMINISTRATION. *A Handbook on Urban Redevelopment for Cities in the United States*. Washington, D.C., 1941.

GALLOWAY, GEORGE B. *Post-war Planning in the United States*. New York, 1942.

GREER, GUY, and HANSEN, ALVIN H. *Urban Redevelopment and Housing*. Washington, D.C., 1941.   .

INTERNATIONAL CITY MANAGERS' ASSOCIATION. *The Municipal Year Book: 1942*. Chicago, 1942.

NATIONAL RESOURCES PLANNING BOARD. *Better Cities*. Washington, D.C., 1942.

———. *Post-war Planning*. Washington, D.C., 1942.

"The Problem of the Cities and Towns." Conference on urbanism, Harvard University, March 5–6, 1942. Cambridge, Mass., 1942.

SERT, J. L. *Can Our Cities Survive?* Cambridge, Mass., 1942.

U.S. BUREAU OF FOREIGN AND DOMESTIC COMMERCE. *Small Town Manual*. Washington, D.C., 1942.

U.S. CONGRESS, HOUSE OF REPRESENTATIVES. *Interstate Migration: Report of the Select Committee To Investigate the Interstate Migration of Destitute Citizens*. Washington, D.C., 1941.

Urban Planning and Public Opinion. National Survey Research Investigation. Princeton, N.J., 1942.

WAGNER, MARTIN, and GROPIUS, WALTER. "Cities' Renaissance," *Kenyon Review*, winter, 1943.

FARMS AND FARMING COMMUNITIES
LOWRY NELSON

✻

W HEN one calls to mind the meagerness of our present knowledge concerning the impact of the first World War on American society, even after twenty-five years of scholarship, one can undertake to analyze the effects of the present war only with a feeling of profound humility. While techniques of observation have improved meanwhile and while there is a more alert awareness on the part of students and of government in recording those observations, the record available to the private individual attempting a current report leaves much to be desired. For example, various government agencies are checking periodically on the status of rural public opinion, but the results are kept confidential and are known to only a limited circle of government employees. However, it is gratifying to know that such records are being kept and will undoubtedly be available for detailed study and analysis after the war.

Indeed, only then can any definitive study of the war's impact be undertaken. In the meantime, we can attempt only a "progress" report based upon data which are published from time to time on such local spot studies as have been made and published and by personal observations and interviews with informed persons.

PRE-WAR AGRICULTURAL DEVELOPMENTS

Since human culture is a continuum rather than a series of discrete segments, it is well to view the impact of a crisis against the perspective of history. As far as American rural society is concerned, a brief résumé of pre-war developments is therefore desirable. Especially significant is the development of social and economic organization among farmers during the last twenty-five years.

During the first twenty years of this century American agriculture occupied the strongest economic position in its history. The farmer's dollar was worth full value in the industrial market place. The demand for farm commodities steadily kept pace with the supply. There were no large surpluses. There was, however, little formal organization among the more than six million farm operators of the country; and the role of the federal government, as far as rural life was concerned, was limited largely to the dissemination of technical information on crop and animal production. Largely as an outgrowth of the recommendations of the Country Life Commission in 1908, the Extension Service under joint federal and state sponsorship was inaugurated in 1914, the year in which the first World War started. In 1916 the federal land banks were created, providing a better system of farm credit than had hitherto been available to farmers. Still there were few controls over economic conditions in agriculture exercised either by government or by the farmers themselves. The economic consequences of the war, in inflated land values and wild speculation, in pushing the frontier of production on to submarginal land, and the inevitable post-war economic collapse are now familiar episodes.

By contrast, the advent of World War II found agriculture organized and operating under controls on a scale previously unknown. The organization of co-operative marketing and purchasing associations among farmers is quite largely a development of the last twenty-five years, while the introduction of federal controls has come about largely in the past decade. These developments represent a response in part to the chronic depression conditions which have affected agriculture since

1920, and which became particularly acute in the early 1930's. The farm depression was the result, on the one hand, of declining demand, particularly of foreign countries, and, on the other, of the steadily increasing productive efficiency resulting from mechanization and improved methods of crop and animal production. The economic depression was coupled with the most severe drought in the history of the country, which, in large areas, created severe destitution and called for further extension of government controls.

A paradox of the rural impoverishment was the fact that large surpluses of many crops were piling up in the country. These surpluses had plagued the markets for many years, and many proposals were put forward to solve the problem. In 1933 the Roosevelt administration created the Agricultural Adjustment Administration, with the object of restoring farm prices through limitation of supply at the source. This meant the restriction of acreage in those crops of which we had excess supplies and the payment of a benefit to farmers for the acreage thus made idle. While the original act was declared unconstitutional, new legislation achieved essentially the same goal through other devices.

Emphasis has been placed upon readjustment of the use of farm land to release from agriculture that which is declared unsuitable and to shift production as far as possible away from surplus crops to those of which there is small or no excess supply, particularly those crops which will conserve and build the soil. The agricultural surpluses have been considered as a national asset and have been placed in storage at government expense through the Ever Normal Granary program. Meantime, a concerted attempt was made through local discussion groups of farmers to acquaint the rural population with the various aspects of the economic problem, particularly the causes of their present difficulty and the details of the program for their alleviation. The farmer today, therefore, is vastly better informed on the operation of the total economy and on his own relations to it. Farmer participation in these controls has been secured also through setting up township, community, county, and state Agricultural Adjustment committees of farmers, who make decisions as to acreage allotments for each unit of organization and for each individual farmer.

Reference to these recent developments in agricultural organization indicates the comparatively different and more favorable situation in which we entered the present war. Agriculture was organized on a national scale, productive efficiency was at a high level, and large supplies of many staple commodities were in the Ever Normal Granary and available to meet new demands at home and abroad. The organization which had been built up made it possible to implement new programs of production with a minimum loss of time.

In considering the repercussions of the war on the farm people of America, the following main topics will be discussed: (*a*) the economic effects; (*b*) changes in rural social organization; (*c*) farmers' attitudes and morale; and (*d*) the outlook for the future.

IMPROVED FARM INCOME

Immediate economic consequences of the war upon the farm have been the most dramatic and most easily perceived. The general effect has been to raise the income of farmers, accompanied by a general acceleration of production, with the latter involving carefully planned operations on a national scale. The national gross farm income for 1942 is estimated by the Department of Agriculture at around fifteen billion dollars. This is more than three times the low record income of $4,700,-000 in 1932 and one-third greater than the income for 1941.[1] This rise in income has enabled the farmers to achieve "par-

[1] *U.S. Department of Agriculture, Agricultural Situation*, XXVI, No. 11 (November, 1942), 3. The net income is forecast at 9.8 billion dollars, the largest on record.

ity" with other segments of the economy for the first time since the last war. Indeed, farm prices in September stood at 109 per cent of parity. In this connection, the question arises as to the possible or probable behavior of farmers as far as the use of income is concerned. For example, will there be another period of inflated land values and an orgy of speculation, such as accompanied the last war? At the moment it appears that this question can be answered in the negative. The Farm Credit Administration reports that the farmers are rapidly liquidating their mortgage indebtedness. The total farm mortgage debt of nearly eleven billion dollars in 1924 has been reduced to around six and one-half billion. The best-informed opinion seems to be that farmers are investing their surplus income in war bonds and insurance premiums in addition to retiring their debts.[2] The events of the last war are still a vivid memory among farmers.

SETTING PRODUCTION GOALS

The mobilization of farmers in meeting production goals was one of the most interesting developments of the past year. But, as already indicated, it did not involve any radical reorganization of the agricultural plant. It was more largely a matter of accelerating the machinery already in motion. Even before the entrance of the United States into the war as an active belligerent, agriculture was being mobilized for increased and planned production under the lend-lease legislation. Plans were oriented particularly to meet the food needs of Britain. These needs are largely pork, eggs, cheese, evaporated milk, dried skim milk, dried beans, and some canned vegetables and processed fruits. These are all products of which we had relatively small surpluses, as compared with

[2] Dorothy S. Brady, "Consumer Spending in 1941–42," *Agricultural Situation*, XXVI, No. 9 (September, 1942), 14.

wheat and cotton, of which we had an extra year's supply. This situation called for stimulated production in livestock and dairy products and for some "retooling" of processing plants, particularly for dehydrating foods.

The events of December, 1941, called for revision upward of production goals. These goals, as Secretary Wickard pointed out, "represented the first effort to draft a comprehensive set of blueprints for all agricultural production in the United States."[3] The more than six million farmers of the United States were asked to adjust their crop and livestock production plans in accordance with the national program. As far as crops are concerned, the plan involved limitation of the acreage of crops of which we already had large supplies, such as the grains and cotton, and greatly expanded acreage of sugar and oil-producing crops (flax, soybeans, peanuts).

Meanwhile, livestock and dairy production was also to be greatly increased. Milk production goals, for example, were increased from 116 billion pounds in 1941 to 125 billion in 1942. This called for increases in the milk-cow population and for better management of dairy herds and care of the milk supply to avoid waste. The other chief animal and animal products which were emphasized in the new production goals were hogs and eggs.

Farmers were encouraged to meet these goals not only by the steadily rising prices but through patriotic appeals consistently carried on by the radio, by the press, and, perhaps more important than all, through personal contacts of agricultural extension workers and state, county, and local war boards and committees with farmers and farm women. While meeting the goals usually involved no sacrifice from a money point of view, it did require the expenditure of a great deal of additional labor on the part of the farmer and his family.

[3] Claude R. Wickard, "Agricultural Supplies for War," *Annals of the American Academy of Political and Social Science*, CCXX (March, 1942), 128.

Patriotic motives undoubtedly played a part in spurring farmers to greater effort.

The final crop report for 1942 of the United States Department of Agriculture showed that the increased food production goals for 1942 were met or exceeded. Total food production was 10 per cent greater than that for 1941, itself a record year. The 1942 production program called for considerable readjustment in the operation of the American farm. In the first place, there was the rearrangement of the cropping system, which in some cases meant the growing of crops with which many farmers had had no previous experience, such as, for example, the production of oil-bearing crops.

DWINDLING LABOR SUPPLY

But the most important problem encountered concerned the supply of farm labor.[4] The labor force in agriculture has for some years been excessive, owing to the decline in agricultural markets, improved farm technology, and the depression in urban industry which inhibited migration from farms. Although the census for 1940 indicated that during the decade of the 1930's there had been practically no change in the number of people living on farms, the Bureau of Agricultural Economics estimated there were 2,500,000 people in excess of labor requirements of agriculture.[5] Part of this excess was due to the aging of the farm population. There was an increase from 1930 to 1940 of about 980,000 people in the farm population of

[4] For excellent statements on the farm labor problem see the Department of Agriculture's *Land Policy Review*, Vol. V, No. 7, containing nine articles by as many authors; and Conrad Taeuber, "Rural Manpower and War Production," testimony before the Select Committee Investigating National Defense Migration, *Washington Hearings, February 12 and 13, 1942*, Part 28. Also the testimony of other competent witnesses in the various volumes issued by the committee.

[5] Division of Farm Population and Rural Welfare, Bureau of Agricultural Economics, "Annual Report, 1941–42" (Washington, D.C., 1942), pp. 15–16. (Mimeographed.)

working age. It should be noted also that the heaviest declines in farm population were on the good farm land of the
nation. Conversely, the increases were noted in the less important agricultural regions, such as the Great Lakes cut-over
areas and in the hilly sections of the South. However, most of
the surplus labor was the result of remarkable improvements
in agricultural technology, including not only mechanization
but the development of improved strains of crops and livestock and new techniques of crop and animal disease control.

That portion of the farm labor supply known as "migratory
labor" has been severely reduced by the tire and car shortage
as well as by the attraction of industrial jobs. While the total
number of these workers constitutes but a small fraction of the
total farm labor force of the nation, they are indispensable to
the operation of large fruit and vegetable farms and, to a considerable extent, of wheat and cotton as well.[6] But they must
be mobile, able to follow the ripening crops as needed. The
Department of Agriculture has made some provision for transporting these workers where private means of travel are not
available; but it appears that the country may need to face the
prospect of severe reduction in supplies of strawberries, let-
tuce, and similar crops. Emphasis is going to have to rest on
the production of staples.

Since the 1940 census appeared, migration from farms has
been accelerated. During 1941, according to estimates made by
the Bureau of Agricultural Economics, there was a net loss to
the farm population through migration of 1,357,000 persons—
the largest for any year since the annual estimates were begun
in 1920.[7] There are no estimates available on a nation-wide

[6] For a brief and excellent account of migratory farm labor see Paul S. Taylor, *Adrift
on the Land* ("Public Affairs Pamphlet," No. 42 [New York: Public Affairs Committee,
1940]). See also n. 4 above.

[7] "Farm Population Estimates," mimeographed release of the U.S. Department of
Agriculture, November, 1942.

scale on the volume of migration during 1942, but that it exceeded 1941 there can be no doubt.[8] Both military and industrial recruitment of farm people—especially men—has been on a much greater scale. During the latter part of 1942 there was nation-wide complaint of farm labor shortages, especially among dairy farmers and fruit and vegetable producers.[9]

The extent of current migration from farms is indicated in several state reports. A survey in North Carolina made during May, 1942, represented a state-wide sample.[10] Information was obtained on the number of men and boys who had left farms for military service or to engage in nonagricultural employment from December 1, 1941, to May 1, 1942. It was estimated that 50,000 workers had migrated from farms during this five-month period, about 45 per cent going into some branch of military service. They constituted 10.5 per cent of all males between fourteen and sixty-five years of age. Nearly three-fifths of the migrants were single men between twenty and forty-five years of age, of whom about two-thirds went into the armed services. Since North Carolina has one of the highest birth rates among the states of the nation, the percentages indicated may not be applicable to other areas. But if even 5 per cent of the male labor force in agriculture has migrated from farms, it would mean a serious depletion of the labor supply in certain areas.

A re-survey of rural youth in Ross County, Ohio, in July, 1942, revealed the fact that, of the rural young men eighteen to twenty-seven years of age who were reported residing in the

[8] Estimates on changes during 1942 will not be available until returns from the annual sample survey which is to be made in January, 1943, are received and tabulated.

[9] The problem of Pacific Coast producers was made especially difficult by the removal of Japanese workers from coast areas.

[10] C. Horace Hamilton and J. T. Wakeley, "Some Effects of the War upon the Farm Labor Situation in North Carolina" (North Carolina Agricultural Experiment Station Special Report [Raleigh, N.C., August 1, 1942]). (Mimeographed.)

county in 1940, only 28 per cent were residing and working in rural Ross County in July, 1942.[11]

On the basis of a reconnaissance survey of the state of Maine, in 1942, Niederfrank estimated that "nearly one-third of the manpower in rural areas . . . . had shifted from local pre-war activities to war industries located elsewhere."[12]

MEETING THE LABOR SHORTAGE

Farmers have met the labor situation in various ways. In the first place, more work has been done by women, the younger children, and the aged, who ordinarily would participate little in outside work on the farm. It was estimated for North Carolina that already women and girls make up about a fifth of the agricultural labor force. On April 1, 1942, the Bureau of Agricultural Economics estimated that, for the country as a whole, 14 per cent of all farm workers were women, compared with the 1940 census figure of 5.8 per cent.

The second means by which farmers met the labor shortage was by more rational planning of farm work. Such jobs as repairs and reconditioning farm equipment—long advocated for winter activity—were probably done on a larger scale than previously. Agricultural extension workers also encouraged farmers to arrange the planting of their crops so that a more even distribution of labor demands could be achieved. This was suggested also on a district basis in the various states in order that there would be a time sequence in the harvesting of the various crops involving large supplies of labor, thus permitting the moving of labor from district to district as the crops came on.

[11] A. R. Mangus, "Loss of Manpower in Rural Ross County, Ohio" (Columbus: Ohio State University, October, 1942). (Mimeographed.)

[12] E. J. Niederfrank, "A Preliminary Survey of the Shift of Manpower in Maine from Rural Areas to Urban War Industrial Centers" (Orono: University of Maine, September, 1942). (Mimeographed.)

A third means employed by farmers was the purchase of additional or better equipment. Fortunately, the supply of equipment and the increased income of farmers made further mechanization possible. Many farmers who had no tractors bought them, while others with older models replaced them with improved machines. Also, through better planning, it was possible to make more efficient utilization of existing equipment. Stocks of farm machinery of many kinds have been completely sold out, some of them months ago.

A fourth device in meeting the labor crisis, and socially the most significant, was through exchange of work among neighbors. Since frontier days farmers have become increasingly self-sufficient as regards labor, largely through the mechanization of agriculture. It is doubtful if at any time since the pioneer period farmers have exchanged labor on so large a scale as has been practiced during the past year. Planning for labor utilization on a neighborhood rather than an individual farm basis has obvious advantages. Slack periods on one farm make it possible to lend labor for a neighboring farm in need of help, which labor can be "returned" at a later period, when it can be used to better advantage. The threshing ring, long an institution among farm folk, has had renewed significance this year. Individual "rings" have been expanded to include more members, even though it has meant the extension of the normal threshing period. At times the neighborly exchange of labor has taxed the planning ingenuity of farmers, often requiring arrangements among three or more individual farms rather than the usual exchange between two farmers.[13]

Finally, "new" sources of farm labor have been tapped,

[13] To some extent, particularly in Wisconsin, there was a transfer of farm people from the less productive lands to work on farms in the better areas. On September 23, in a statement before the House Committee on Agriculture, Secretary Wickard urged this translocation of farmers to meet the labor needs for 1943. Should this be practiced on a large scale, it would be one of the most important wartime developments in American agriculture.

chiefly in the form of city and town young people and men, who have responded to the call for help. People of many rural towns (merchants, tradesmen, professionals) agreed to make their services available to farmers when and if needed to bring in the crops. Through the United States Employment Service, many city youngsters were placed in jobs on farms. While such labor is often of limited value because of inexperience in farm work, there can be no doubt that it has helped greatly to fill the gap left by the migration of the regular farm workers.[14]

In California a state-wide registration of school children available for farm work was undertaken by the State Department of Education as an aid in helping to mobilize all available labor for agricultural needs. In practically all sections of the country workers on relief and W.P.A. were utilized to the maximum degree possible.

In addition to these sources of farm labor, Japanese evacuated from the Pacific Coast have been employed to some extent in sugar-beet harvesting, and there has been a limited number of workers imported from Mexico and from Canada under special international agreements.

GOVERNMENT AIDS

The government has rendered considerable direct aid in a number of ways. In the first place, the work of the Employment Service has been greatly extended, and farmers have been urged to use this service to the maximum. This is a significant development in view of the fact that the farm labor market has historically been characterized by chaotic conditions. Labor has been recruited on a hit-and-miss basis, and labor itself by the same token has had to seek its own jobs as best it could with little or no guidance. Coupled with the federal Employment Service is governmental provision for transporting do-

---

[14] For a story in popular form as to how this kind of labor was utilized see Frank J. Taylor, "Dude Harvest," *Saturday Evening Post*, October 3, 1942.

mestic farm labor from one section to another, as the need is certified by the Employment Service. In undertaking this transport service, the government, through the Manpower Commission, will specify certain minimum conditions of employment, including payment of the prevailing wage with a minimum wage of 30 cents an hour, guaranty of employment for at least 75 per cent of the working time in the contract period, adequate housing, health, and sanitary facilities, prohibition of child labor under fourteen years of age, and some other conditions.[15]

The Farm Security Administration, with its ninety-five labor camps, has made an important contribution to the effective distribution of the available labor supply.

CHANGES IN RURAL SOCIAL ORGANIZATION

The war has brought a number of new committees and organizations to the rural community and, more important, a new official use of natural social areas. As is well known, rural people are not ordinarily residents of incorporated governmental units. Group identity has been with informal neighborhood areas, the town-country community areas, or simply with the township—where these exist as legal entities. Neighborhoods are undoubtedly the most important of the "natural social areas," although they have been used surprisingly little by governmental agencies in the past. During the war period, however, there has been for the first time a nation-wide program to organize rural effort on a neighborhood basis. Rural sociologists have developed a simple mapping technique, usable by county extension workers and volunteer farm committees, by which these natural local areas can be delineated.

On the basis of these delineated neighborhoods, committees of farm men and women have been set up to function in connection with the food production program and other phases of the

[15] News release, U.S. Department of Agriculture, August 20, 1942.

war. This may well prove to be a development of lasting significance.[16] A survey in Massachusetts showed that "farm families contacted by the neighborhood leaders made much greater response to the [agricultural] program than farm families not contacted."[17]

In connection with activities involving town and country co-operation, committees are organized on the basis of the trade-area community, using again in practice a concept developed by Dr. C. J. Galpin in 1915 and subsequently elaborated by rural sociologists working in various states and the federal government. It is not improbable that, as a result of these developments, farmers may become more fully integrated into the trade-area community.

But the county perhaps will remain as the key unit for the organization of rural effort, and the war has brought some changes or additions on this level. In 1941 the state and county agricultural war boards were organized, the special function of which was the implementation of the war effort as far as agriculture was concerned. In many states subcommittees of the war boards on farm labor, machinery rationing, and transportation were set up on both the county and the state levels.

RURAL SCHOOLS

Among rural social institutions, rural schools have probably been most severely affected by the war. The most serious disturbance is the creation of a teacher shortage, chiefly as a result of the migration of women teachers—who constitute the vast majority of the rural personnel—to better-paid positions in industry and in government service. Since rural salaries

[16] This point is suggested by Bryce Ryan and C. Arnold Anderson in a very interesting article, "Changes in Rural Life Growing Out of the War," *Rural Sociology*, VII, No. 3 (September, 1942), 239 ff.

[17] "Evaluation Study of the Neighborhood Leader System, Berkshire and Essex Counties, Mass., May, 1942" (Department of Agriculture Extension Service Circ. 386 [Washington, D.C., July, 1942]). (Mimeographed.)

have been notoriously low, the disparity between them and the extraordinary wages paid in industry and even in government service is very great. The situation is made more acute by the fact that for several years past there has been a shortage of personnel in this field. The Selective Service Act has also helped to deplete the ranks of the male rural teachers, although this has not been a serious factor because of the low percentage of males in the rural teaching force.

How serious the teacher shortage is cannot be told with accuracy at this time. As early as May, 1942, twenty states reported shortages of rural teachers, and only two reported surpluses.[18]

On the high-school level a recent report from the Office of Education showed that in August, 1942, thirty-eight states reported the closing of 602 departments of vocational agriculture due to lack of teachers.[19] In the same month the state superintendent of public instruction for Michigan estimated the closing of as many as one thousand rural schools in that state alone.[20] The Office of Education forecast a shortage of fifty thousand rural teachers for the country at large. States in which war industries are very significant have suffered most in this respect.

As to the situation of rural schools since the opening of the school year, the following statement from the Office of Education represents the latest information available:

This Office is just now completing the tabulation of data secured from a Nation-wide survey of teacher shortage. I regret that copies of the report are not now available. However, earlier predictions of a serious shortage have been confirmed. The shortage varies among States, among school systems within States, and among the subjects and grade levels taught. The shortage indicated in your letter has

---

[18] U.S. Office of Education, *Education for Victory*, I, No. 12 (August, 15, 1942), 15.

[19] *Ibid.*, No. 17 (November 2, 1942), 19.

[20] *Chicago Tribune*, August 15, 1942.

been met in part by issuing emergency certificates and otherwise lowering certification requirements, employing married women and other teachers out of service for some time, use of young or of inexperienced teachers, and similar means. Standards of teacher employment, as well as of certification, have been lowered. Nevertheless, there were between 8,000 and 10,000 unfilled teaching vacancies for which teachers were still being sought last October 15. There was an estimated 138,000 new teachers, many more than in previous years. The worst shortages were in rural schools, and in special and vocational war-related high school subjects, such as industrial arts, physical education for men, physics, mathematics, agriculture, chemistry, commercial education and the like. There were large numbers of schools and subject departments closed; but inasmuch as many rural schools are closed by consolidation even in normal times, it is not believed that a figure on "closed schools" is as significant as it might be.[21]

This depletion of the ranks of rural teachers and the consequent closing of some schools do not necessarily mean that a corresponding number of rural children will go without school opportunities this year. Part of the vacancies will be filled by married women who were former schoolteachers and who may be granted emergency teaching certificates. In the second place, those children who would have normally attended the schools which had to be closed may be transported to near-by schools. It should be pointed out, however, that such transportation is limited by the availability of tires and gasoline, and this may result in rather serious deprivation of educational opportunity before the war is over. Given adequate transportation, the accelerated consolidation of rural schools might be regarded as a favorable development.

To meet the situation it has been strongly urged by responsible bodies that salaries to rural teachers be increased through higher local levies for school purposes, increased state aid, and

---

[21] From a letter to the writer from Benjamin W. Frazier, senior specialist in teacher-training, Office of Education, January 21, 1943.

the adoption of a program of federal aid; the consolidation of school districts where feasible; the provision by state departments for emergency certification of teachers; and provision for refresher and in-service training courses.[22]

Already, rural schools are adapting the teaching program to war needs by giving additional emphasis to health instruction and nutrition; to governmental relations, domestic and international; and in performing many war services, such as distribution of rationing cards, participation in salvage operations, and the like. By and large, it is possible that the schools will become community centers to a degree never before realized.

In many sections where farm labor shortage is critical the schools are shortening their terms by holding school on Saturdays, in order to release students during heavy farm operation in the spring and fall.

FARM ATTITUDES AND MORALE

Like most of the American population, farmers faced the prospect of another war with mixed emotions. While any generalizations are fraught with uncertainty, it is probably safe to say that prior to Pearl Harbor there were some broad differences between farmers of the North and those of the South. The rural South is more homogeneous from the standpoint of its nationality origins and in its party politics. The fact that there were few people in the South whose ancestors came from countries with whom we are at war meant that this factor at least did not constitute an impediment to their supporting the pre–Pearl Harbor policies. Moreover, the fact that they largely belong to the political party in power was a further factor in making it emotionally possible for them to support the foreign policies of the government.

[22] See, e.g., *The Rural Child in the War Emergency* (Chicago: Committee on Rural Education [5835 Kimbark Ave.], 1942).

In the North we have the contrasting situation of diverse nationality groups, with large numbers of German origin. But there are also considerable numbers of those who descend from European countries which have been overrun and subjugated by the German armies. While it would be dangerous to overemphasize the importance of the nationality factor in conditioning the attitudes of people toward the war, it would be equally unwise to fail to recognize it as a possible influence on morale. In so far as it has conditioned behavior among farm people, it would be of vastly greater importance in the North.

Since a large portion of northern farmers have been traditionally Republican as far as party politics are concerned, they would have more reservations than would southerners in supporting the foreign policies of the government. Also because of the composite character of the northern population, nationalistic sentiments are probably less pronounced than in the South.

Nevertheless, such isolationist sentiment as existed among farmers before the Japanese attack was largely dissipated by that event. For those who may still decry our entrance into the European phase of the conflict, it is possible now for them to resolve their emotional conflicts by defining the situation as a war against Japan. I do not wish to give the impression that there is any significant defection among those nationality groups with whose native countries we are now at war. On the contrary, there is ample evidence that they are responding patriotically to the American war effort. Space will not permit the inclusion of such evidence as has come to the attention of the writer.

The food-for-victory program of the Department of Agriculture must be credited as an important factor in raising and sustaining farmer morale. Its effectiveness lay in the specific answer which it gave every farmer to the question: "What can I

do to help?'' The production goals were concrete and were interpreted to each farmer in terms of acres and bushels, number
of hogs, and amount of milk he should contribute as his share
of the total effort. The farmers were given their allotments by
committees of their neighbors. All the while the Department
of Agriculture, through press and radio, was pointing out the
important role which farmers would play in the total war
effort. "Food will win the war and write the peace," said one
of the slogans. Farmers, therefore, became important in their
own eyes in terms of the contribution they could make to the
national welfare.

There is one other point in connection with farmer attitudes which needs to be mentioned. That concerns their reaction to price control. The behavior of the farm bloc in the
national Congress and of the legislative representatives of
some of the national farm organizations might give the impression that the farmers were seeking to "feather their nests"
at the expense of the war program. As far as I have been able
to check the situation, grass-roots sentiment is not in line with
sentiments as expressed by the farm bloc. Farmers do not want
any bonus for their contribution to the war. They are not asking for anything above parity prices. I think it is true to say,
however, that the most damaging factor to farmer morale is
the payment of such high wages and profits in industry as to
give nonfarm segments of the population an unreasonable re-
ward for their contribution. All the farmer asks is assurance
that the total burden is being equitably shared. In this respect, he is not any different from the rest of the population.
He regards present wage levels in war industries as unreason-
ably high and as one of the chief factors in making it impossible for him to secure adequate labor, since he cannot hope to
compete in the labor market against such odds. Nevertheless,
he has a great fear of inflation, born of his sad experience in the

last war, and would not want to stand in the way of any program destined to forestall it.

SUMMARY

By way of summary, the net effects of the war on American agriculture and rural society have been these:

1. It has brought to farmers the largest aggregate income in history.

2. The tempo of productive activity has greatly increased.

3. Certain readjustments have been made in the crop and livestock systems, an achievement which was greatly simplified by the existence of a nation-wide organization of agriculture under government direction.

4. Some new agencies such as war boards, neighborhood committees, and the like have come into being in response to the war situation. Often, however, too little consideration has been given to the possibility of utilizing existing machinery in the rural community; while many of these special war agencies will no doubt disappear when peace comes, there is a possibility that the neighborhood system may remain as a permanent residue.

5. There has been an extension of neighborhood relations in the matter of exchange of work and machinery and possibly a closer integration of farm and nonfarm people in the rural community. This is largely a response to the labor shortage.

6. The impact of war on the rural school has been immediate and severe, but seriousness varies in degree among regions of the country.

7. Farmer morale is "high" but is threatened by the disparity between industrial and farm wages.

THE OUTLOOK FOR THE FUTURE

It requires no prophetic insight to discern certain important developments in the year ahead, assuming a continuation of the war through the coming crop year. Already the labor situation is acute and growing worse by the day. Particularly serious is the dwindling supply of year-round labor to man the dairy farms. Since dairying requires a degree of skill that comes only from experience, it is practically impossible to replace the men called to the armed services and entering industrial employment from this part of the farm enterprise. Moreover, they cannot be replaced entirely by machinery, since the source of new equipment has been reduced. The situation has been fully discussed in the press of the country in recent months, and the prospect of a selective service program for labor is coming steadily closer to realization. It has been suggested that if worse comes to worse we devote the available productive factors in agriculture to the production of those commodities with the greatest caloric value in terms of labor input.

However, there is still unused labor in rural areas. Many small, marginal farmers might be shifted from areas of low productivity per man to the more promising sections where their labor can be most adequately utilized. Moreover, farmers have not used available farm machinery as fully as might be done. Farmers are reluctant to lend or rent machinery to their neighbors in view of the present outlook for replacements.

If the present rate of migration of teachers from rural areas continues, the situation of the rural schools next year will indeed be critical. Enrolment in teacher-training institutions has been declining for two years past at least, so that even the usual supply of teachers from this source will progressively diminish.

It is not difficult either to see further serious depletion in the ranks of rural medical personnel, both doctors and nurses. For many years past there has been a distinct drift away from rural practice on the part of physicians—a drift which the war will no doubt greatly accelerate.

Farmers have depended increasingly on the automobile for access to services of health, education, and other social and economic agencies. Should this means of transportation be further restricted, serious consequences are easily foreseen.

Farm people, as well as the population in general, will face the critical impact of the war for the first time [1943]. Up to the present time, relatively few civilians have made any real personal sacrifices for the war. Some small industries and retailers have no doubt suffered, as have some of those on fixed salaries. But farmers as a class, along with laborers and entrepreneurs in war industries, have been the beneficiaries of a considerable war boom. No real sacrifices, made out of devotion to the common cause, have been required. As the heavy burden of taxation and possible compulsory purchase of war bonds dig deep into the farm income, as it becomes more difficult to get the things needed or desired in family living, as more homes are called upon to suffer the loss of close relatives on the battle front, and as more severe government controls further limit personal freedom, then, and only then, will the tensile strength of rural morale be fully tested. These experiences appear inevitable in 1943.

BIBLIOGRAPHY

Brady, Dorothy. "Consumer Spending in 1941–42," *Agricultural Situation*, XXVI, No. 9 (September, 1942), 11–14.

Committee on Rural Education. *The Rural Child in the War Emergency*. Chicago, 1942.

Dickens, Dorothy. "What War Is Doing to the Farm Family," *Journal of Home Economics*, XXXIV (June, 1942), 358–61.

National Education Association, Educational Policies Committee. *A War Policy for American Schools*. Washington, D.C., February, 1942.

Raper, Arthur, and Forsyth, F. Howard. "Cultural Factors Which Result in Artificial Farm Labor Shortages," *Rural Sociology*, VII, No. 1 (March, 1943), 3–14.

RYAN, BRYCE, and ANDERSON, C. ARNOLD, "Changes in Rural Life Growing Out of the War," *Rural Sociology*, VII, No. 3 (September, 1942), 239 ff.

TAYLOR, C. C. "Rural Life," *American Journal of Sociology,* XLVII, No. 6 (May, 1942), 841–53. (Discussion of recent pre-war changes in rural society.)

TAYLOR, PAUL S. *Adrift on the Land.* "Public Affairs Pamphlet," No. 42. New York, 1940.

U.S. CONGRESS, HOUSE OF REPRESENTATIVES. *Hearings of Select Committee Investigating National Defense Migration: Washington Hearings, February 12 and 13, 1942* (77th Cong., 2d sess.). (Contains valuable testimony regarding farm labor.)

U.S. DEPARTMENT OF AGRICULTURE, BUREAU OF AGRICULTURAL ECONOMICS. "Farm Population Estimates, 1910–1942." Washington, D.C., 1942. (Mimeographed.)

U.S. DEPARTMENT OF AGRICULTURE. *Land Policy Review* (Washington, D.C.), Vol. V, No. 7 (fall, 1942). (Series of nine articles by various authors on farm labor.)

U.S. OFFICE OF EDUCATION. *Education for Victory*, I, No. 12 (August 15, 1942), 15. (Shortages and surpluses by various categories of teachers for May, 1942.)

———. "Teacher Losses and Supply in Vocational Agriculture," *ibid.*, No. 17 (November 2, 1942), 19.

WELLS, ORIS V. "Our Changing Food Consumption," *Agricultural Situation*, XXVI, No. 8 (August, 1942), 15 ff.

WICKARD, CLAUDE R. "Agricultural Supplies for War," *Annals of the American Academy of Political and Social Science*, Vol. CCXX (March, 1942).

SOCIAL SCIENCE AND THE SOLDIER

SAMUEL A. STOUFFER

THE Army has been called "the cutting edge of American democracy" by General MacArthur. The job of the soldier is to kill. His training has a single ultimate purpose—to destroy the enemy. But only a fraction of the armed forces in any country will meet their enemy in face-to-face death grip. Most of the soldiers will be behind the fighting front, either in the long lines of supply and communications or patrolling areas remote from the combat zone.

Thus the function of many of the soldiers becomes almost indistinguishable from the function of millions of civilians at various stages in the production lines, all of which converge in the man who bares his breast to the enemy. It is like an expedition to conquer the summit of Mount Everest. Only a handful of men will make camp at the upper altitudes, and even fewer will be assigned to the task of reaching the top. But below that, at camp after camp, will be many upon whom the rest depend.

In speaking of the Army in modern, total war, it is important to keep in mind the fact that, except for the wearing of a uniform and the regimentation of military life, there is little to distinguish the functions and problems of many of the soldiers and civilians.

This similarity has other aspects. Many morale problems are shared in common. Let us illustrate, in some detail, with the problem of orientation as to the aims of the war. A man's orientation may be described in terms of three factors: (1) the clarity of his conception of the aims of the collective effort; (2) the evaluation he places on these aims; and (3) the degree to which he identifies his personal aims with the collective aims. Pearl Harbor brought unanimity on at least this point: Our side, whatever the reason, has been attacked, and we darned well better not find ourselves on the losing side at the end. Possibly this is motivation enough, but it could hardly be argued that the motivation would not be stronger if the aims of the collective effort could be crystallized as sharply as in World War I and as closely identified with the personal aims of the individual.

There is much cynicism to overcome. Most men of military age grew up in the midst of disillusionment about the Great Crusade of a generation ago, and their conception of the American way we are fighting to defend includes, inevitably, many bitter memories of a decade of depression. The entire job experience of most young men was in the depths of depression, except as the war boom began to bring them sudden prosperity —from which millions were abruptly separated in order to don a uniform.

How extensive these developments are, what specified forms they take, and what the effects of measures taken to overcome them are—all these are problems for research not only in the Army but also in civilian life.

TWO ASPECTS OF THE RELATIONSHIP OF SOCIAL SCIENCE TO WAR PROBLEMS

In discussing problems of the soldiers, I should like to take the liberty of limiting the discussion rather narrowly. Here in this building dedicated to social science research it is particularly appropriate if we confine ourselves to considering two questions: (1) What is social science contributing to sharpening "the cutting edge of American democracy"? (2) What can social science expect to learn as a by-product of this practical honing job? In fact, I should like to limit the subject even further. Instead of speaking about social science in general, I should prefer rather to speak mainly of the social scientist trained in sociology or psychology, leaving to others the consideration of the contributions of history, economics, political science, and other disciplines.

PSYCHOLOGY SINCE WORLD WAR I

In World War I a distinguished American psychologist was asked, "What can psychology contribute to winning the war?" He is reported to have replied, "Nothing." He was, of course, quite wrong. World War I marked the first large-scale application of psychological tests of intelligence and vocational aptitudes. The impact of this work on psychology after the war was of tremendous importance, and techniques of psychological measurement subsequently made their influence felt everywhere in education and in industry. This work also paved the way for new approaches in psychological theory. The work of Dr. L. L. Thurstone and his colleagues at the University of Chicago, and of scores of others who are laboring in the development of quantitative psychological theories, rests upon the cultural base of hundreds of man-years of experience in test construction which was given its greatest impetus in the crises of World War I. This development in the measurement of intelligence and vocational aptitudes is bearing rich, practical fruit in our Army and Navy today.

SOCIAL PSYCHOLOGY AND SOCIOLOGY SINCE WORLD WAR I

At the time of World War I social psychology and sociology, as the journals of that period will show, had not advanced particularly far beyond the essay stage. Theories flourished, but it was the practice to illustrate them with examples somewhat as a preacher illustrates his sermons rather than to submit the ideas to empirical tests. There was a great deal of bandying-about of the word "science," but one does not need to engage in a controversy on the definition of science to say that at least one of the important elements of science, namely, verification, was usually missing.

The two decades after the Treaty of Versailles have been decades of unprecedented advance in sociology and social psychology. A serious effort has been made to phrase some of the theories in forms permitting at least beginnings of scientific verification. At the same time, the techniques developed by statisticians, anthropologists, psychoanalysts, and others have been refined. It would be silly to say that, when the Japanese struck at Pearl Harbor, social psychologists and sociologists were ready with a set of theories and techniques perfectly adapted for aiding the Army. But it is true that the accumulated experience of years of patient work has given the sociologist and social psychologist an opportunity in the war effort which he could not have taken advantage of two decades ago.

Those of us who happen to be assigned to work on problems of the soldier are, of course, only a small fraction of the sociologists and psychologists who are devoting their professional skills to the winning of the war. As I indicated at the beginning, many of the problems of the soldier and the civilian, of the Army and of industry, have large elements in common, and there is need for the widest possible exchange of ideas among us all.

THE ARMY'S RESPONSIBILITIES TO THE NEW RECRUIT

When a man is taken out of civilian life and put into uniform, the Army has at least four responsibilities: (1) to fit him into an Army job which, if possible, uses his civilian skills and vocational aptitudes and interests to a maximum; (2) to teach him the specialized trade of war; (3) to guard his health; and (4) to sustain his morale.

Classification.—The responsibility for developing methods of testing and classification which will fit the right man into the right job is one which has been handled ably by psychologists who are experts in test construction and occupational classification. Hundreds of psychologists are working in the ground forces and in the air forces on the development and application of classification tests. These tests did not always work well at first. This was partly because some of the tests were imperfect, especially in the field of vocational aptitudes; but even more important is the fact that a long period of education has been necessary to make commanding officers aware of the importance of using these test results in assigning men. Classification and assignment are like two blades of a pair of scissors. One can say that the classification blade is now keen and sharp and that the assignment blade is getting sharper as officers have come to appreciate the importance of correct assignment. I shall not speak more of this very important work now but refer to it again in connection with the relation of job assignment to morale.

Training.—After the Army has classified the recruit and given him his Army assignment, there is the problem of teaching him the trade of war. The Army, like all society, has gone through an industrial revolution, and the different kinds of tasks which different people learn as part of their instruction in the trade of war run into the thousands. Thus far, it cannot be said that the social psychologist, as such, has been in the position to make much of a direct contribution to the training program. Training for war is a profession, and the leaders of the military profession have developed, over decades of experience, many standardized training techniques. Nevertheless, one finds in high places in the Army many inquiring minds who doubt that a method is adequate simply because it is honored by custom. These men have shown ingenuity and organizational ability in applying mass-production methods to education in certain areas relatively new in warfare, particularly those involving the use of machines. Some of the teaching devices introduced, particularly motion pictures, are likely to have a lasting effect on educational techniques. It is remarkable, for example, what Walt Disney can do as a pedagogue.

Health.—It is hard to conceive how any Army could have taken more care with the health and physical well-being of its soldiers than the American Army of today. In securing thousands of younger doctors in their thirties and forties, the Army has undoubtedly availed itself of medical skill with better scientific training than that of the average physician and surgeon in the general population. The regularity of habits, the hard physical exercises, and the abundant food in the Army make for tough bodies. The clothing and shelter of the average soldier are far superior to that of a generation ago. The venereal disease rate has been kept within bounds. The rapidity with which our citizen Army had to be built made the problem of adequate screening of psychiatric cases difficult, but there is awareness of the problem and a determination to profit by the lessons of the last war. It is too early to evaluate the contributions which psychiatry will make in this war.

Morale.—Finally, the Army has the problem not only of finding the right Army job for a man, teaching him the trade of war, and safeguarding his health but also of sustaining what, for want of a better word, is usually called "morale." As the saying goes in the Army, morale is a function of command. By that it is meant that every commanding officer down to the company commander is held responsible for the morale of the troops below him. This must be understood in order to appreciate how the social psychologist who is brought into work with the Army can make his influence felt.

A staff officer in Washington, working on the problem of arming the mind and spirit of the soldier, has definite limits to his action. His plans must be approved by and transmitted through the chain of command, which means that in many respects he can advise but not execute. However, he does have at least one route of direct impact upon the soldier through his influence on the principal military agencies of communication and information to the soldier.

ORGANIZATION OF MORALE ACTIVITIES

It was fortunate for the Army that as head of the morale activities there was appointed a leader of American business who, by his authorship of two volumes in the field of social science, had demonstrated his concern for the application of scientific knowledge to the problems of human relations. This man is Brigadier General Frederick H. Osborn, a member of the Social Science Research Council and a trustee of the Carnegie Corporation.

General Osborn has two main responsibilities. The first is to make plans for the utilization of a soldier's leisure time, to train officers to direct leisure-time activities, to provide recreational, musical, and library equipment, and to serve as a liaison with civilian agencies such as the Red Cross and the U.S.O. His second main responsibility is to provide information to troops. This he is doing through supervision of the production, in Hollywood, of motion-picture films; through the preparation of short-wave broadcasts and phonograph transcriptions for troops overseas; through supervision of a weekly Army magazine available to all soldiers; through assistance to hundreds of local camp newspapers; through the preparation of educational booklets to be read by soldiers on transports, describing the customs of the land to which they are sailing; through the preparation of foreign-language records which will teach men to speak needed key words in the language of the land of their destination; through the preparation of lectures and discussions—in fact, through every medium by which it is possible to inform and inspire our fighting men and those in training or in the services of supply.

An Army Institute has been established to provide correspondence courses primarily for the hundreds of thousands of men who may be frustrated at isolated posts, and a foundation is now being laid for an adult education program which should be of tremendous significance in what may be a long-drawn-out demobilization period after victory is won.

The role of research in morale activities.—General Osborn believes in research. Slowly, he has built up in Washington a staff of sociologists and psychologists who operate under directives from the chief of staff to study problems of the soldier, not only in order to provide guidance to General Osborn but also to be of service to any branch of the Army which wants assistance.

Many and varied are the problems presented to the research staff. What kind of orientation is necessary to build the most effective fighting morale? Under what conditions is hatred of the enemy or fear a desirable motivation? Should we laugh at Mussolini? What factors in Army life tend to undermine the will to fight? Should the amenities with which the soldier in training is provided be curtailed and should he start in with the same Spartan scale of living as his fellows in Guadalcanal? Or, as long as he has leaves and furloughs and sees his civilian friends enjoying the fruits of high wages, should he get, as far as possible, the best of everything? Under what conditions is "griping" in camp a healthy sign and under what conditions is it an unhealthy sign? Are there some conditions calling for tough, hardboiled leadership and others calling for fatherly leadership of soldiers? What already favorably existing attitudes can be exploited to overcome prejudices against some of our allies?

Similarly, what about the prejudices against the high wages of civilian labor? What predictions can be made about the kind of personality which will break down on the battlefield or at isolated outposts? What predictions can be made about the kind of personality which will make a good noncommissioned officer? What basis is there for thinking either that it is better to keep officers and men from the same communities together in the same outfit or better to disperse them? How about men of the same national origin, or men of about the same social class, or about the same intelligence level? How can the prestige of noncombat troops be built up?

Questions like these, challenging to the sociologist and social psychologist and frequently unanswerable even with the use of the cleverest of techniques of investigation, are mixed with other questions of a more mundane character. What proportion of men complain that their pants don't fit? What suggestions do the men have for improving the service at U.S.O. clubs? How many boys drink beer on a typical Saturday night?

Questions and problems differ depending on the zone of operations of the soldier. The soldier in training at home has different problems from the soldier on duty at remote and quiet bases on the Pacific islands, Alaska, Iceland, the Caribbean, and other isolated parts of the world. Still different are the problems of the noncombat soldier in the zones of active fighting. Finally, of course, special classes of problems pertain to the man with the gun face-to-face with the enemy in North Africa or wherever the battlefields may be.

Research work: surveys.—The work done by this research staff falls into two categories: (1) surveys and (2) experimental studies.

Methods have been worked out, after a good deal of trial and error, of questioning enlisted men in an atmosphere of anonymity which produces frank and earnest answers. The research staff has made studies in about eighty-five camps in the Army ground forces and air forces in continental United States and at several overseas bases.

The studies have covered a wide range of topics. For example, it was desired to know how men in the infantry were reacting to the constant flood of publicity, much of it irresponsible, about the futility of infantrymen in an age of mechanized warfare. Careful sets of questions were prepared, and infantrymen of all types were interviewed. Working in collaboration with psychologists in the office of the adjutant general, who are responsible for constructing intelligence and aptitude tests, the research staff has made extensive studies of the problems of job classification and assignment in the Army. These studies uncovered some discontent and pointed to ways of remedying it.

Attempts have been made to classify the chief points of frustration felt by the soldiers in training. Tests and scales have been developed to measure, as quickly and as accurately as possible, the extent of these frustrations. The resulting information has been submitted to the policy-makers—in some cases with important effects on Army policy.

A year ago [1941] the most frustrated group in the Army was that of the well-educated soldiers, many of whom felt they were not getting a chance to show what they could do. This situation was quite understandable. The educational level of the selectees was much higher than that of the old regular Army enlisted men; but the latter, because of experience, were necessarily serving as teachers of the new recruits and as advisers to company commanders with respect to promotions. Time and changes in Army policy have gone a long way toward solving this problem. Many men are still frustrated, but the well-educated man now, if he has the requisite intelligence and leadership qualities, has an excellent chance to go to Officers' Candidate School and obtain a commission.

New recruits coming into the Army bring with them, of course, attitudes toward the war and toward our allies which are the result of the education and information that they, like other civilians, received through the public schools, the press, the radio, and other agencies of communication. These attitudes can be measured and, by applying theories of social psychology and various quantitative techniques, can be described with sufficient explicitness to serve as a valuable guide to those in charge of the information and education of the soldier.

Research work: experimental studies.—The research work is not confined to surveys. In addition, there is being carried on a systematic program of actual experimental studies. The idea of controlled experiments is not new in the Army. It is used routinely in testing new weapons and other articles of equipment. But it is perhaps a new, and somewhat exciting, development to see the experimental methods of natural science applied by the Army in the field of social psychology.

A motion-picture film especially prepared, let us say, to create better understanding of one of our allies is believed to have six determinable objectives. The research staff designs a technique for measuring the degree to which each objective has been attained. Two matched groups of men are pretested; one group sees the film, and a control group does not. Both groups are restudied after a week or two, thus making it possible to measure how much influence the film has had with respect to each of the predetermined objectives. Many modifications can be and have been introduced in designing the experiments. For example, a third group can see the film, followed by an informal discussion. The time interval can be varied. With the help of these results, advice can be given about needed changes in film material or about emphases which need to be made in the new films yet to be produced.

This is one of the special fields in which experimental studies have been made or are in preparation. In quite another area considerable experimental work has been done on physical conditioning, with a view to measuring effects produced by attempts to improve the physical training. Extensive preparatory work is also under way on the subject of fear, again drawing on the best social psychological knowledge available and attempting to provide a better scientific basis for teaching methods of controlling fear.

In the process of carrying out this work, the research staff has made some progress in the development of improved instruments of measurement which may be of considerable importance to research in social psychology and sociology in the future. A new theory of scale construction, for example, developed out of practical needs, has given promise of wide utility.

THE SOCIAL SCIENTIST IN AN ARMY MILIEU

Research reports in the Army, because of the nature of the work, are usually confidential. This imposes an extraordinary responsibility. A report in sociology or social psychology which is read at a scholarly meeting or published in a scholarly journal is always subject to the white heat of academic criticism. Many are the battles that have been fought over what purports to be a contribution to social science. Nothing can quite take the place of this safeguard against the inaccurate and the spurious. However, any piece of research turned out by the staff of Special Service must run quite a gantlet of internal criticism and usually must pass the inspection of one or more outside critics who are sworn in as special consultants and whose responsibility it is to be as devastating as possible.

In the Washington mêleé one cannot keep the Alpine detachment which is the glory of university research in times of peace. There are many frustrations. Questions are asked which cannot now be answered. The war cannot wait on science if science is not ready and often pays no attention even if science does have something to contribute. An Army man is often justified in his suspicions of the academician. A hundred and one housekeeping problems drain off research energy which should go into clear thinking. All the agencies doing work in sociology or social psychology, such as the Office of

War Information, Office of Strategic Services, Military Intelligence, and others, have much the same experience.

Yet, amid the disappointments, the blockings, the failures, there is a solid sense of satisfaction among those of us devoted to social science when we see the accumulated research experience of our scientific disciplines operate to sharpen a little keener that "cutting edge of American democracy," now flashing into action on every continent to preserve what we hold dear.

BIBLIOGRAPHY

American Journal of Sociology, Vol. XLVII, No. 3 (November, 1941), issue on "National Morale."

Annals of the American Academy of Political and Social Science, Vol. CCXX (March, 1942), issue on "Organizing for Total War," especially: BINGHAM, WALTER V., "The Army Personnel Classification System," pp. 18–28; OSBORN, FREDERICK H., "Recreation, Welfare, and Morale of the American Soldier," pp. 50–56.

BINGHAM, WALTER V., "Psychological Services in the Army," *Journal of Consulting Psychology*, V (1941), 221 ff.

CHILD, IRVIN L. "Morale: A Bibliographical Survey," *Psychological Bulletin*, XXXVI, No. 6 (June, 1941), 393–420.

COMMITTEE ON CLASSIFICATION OF PERSONNEL IN THE ARMY. *The Personnel System of the U.S. Army*, Vol. I: *History of the Personnel System;* Vol. II: *The Personnel Manual*. Washington, 1919.

COMMITTEE FOR NATIONAL MORALE. *German Psychological Warfare*. New York, 1941.

FAUBION, RICHARD W., and BELLOWS, ROGER M. "Personnel Work in the Army Air Forces: The Classification Division, Army Air Forces Technical Training Command," *Psychological Bulletin*, XXXIX, No. 8 (October, 1942), 643–64.

MUNSON, EDWARD L. *The Management of Men*. New York, 1921.

Psychiatry: Journal of the Biology and Pathology of Interpersonal Relations, Vol. IV, No. 2 (May, 1941), articles on role of psychiatrists in the Selective Service System.

YOAKUM, C. S., and YERKES, R. M. *Army Mental Tests*. New York, 1920.

THE ROLE OF THE CITIZEN

ELLSWORTH FARIS

✿

AMERICA is fighting a war with soldiers on what one writer counted as thirty-four fronts. Fighting men are being equipped to battle in the ice of the Arctic, the hot sands of the desert, the jungles of the Tropics, and the mountain country of all the continents. Accurately named "total," rightly called "global," the whole of the planet is at war, with the exception of the few neutral nations who are neither great nor strong and can be counted on one's fingers. We are all-out. In extent and in severity this is a war the like of which has never been seen since history was first written.

Ceaseless iteration has made Americans fully conscious of the vital part that the citizen plays in this total war. While the soldier and the sailor fight, the munition worker is equally essential, the farm laborer rightly feels that he is no less important, the railroad brakeman feels that he is helping to win the war, the housewife aids by conserving food and limiting her purchases, and the children collecting tin cans have a sense of partnership in the mightiest effort the nation has ever made. We are all-out.

MORALE IS UNPRECEDENTEDLY HIGH

Our people are determined to win the war and are certain that we shall be victorious. The word "morale" is sometimes loosely used, but if by morale is meant the confidence that we shall be able to overcome our enemies, then it is safe to say that no country ever had higher morale. If by defeatism is meant the view or feeling or sentiment that expects us to lose the war, then defeatism seems impossible to find in any corner of the land or among any segment of our people. Criticism and conflict can exist concerning the ways of fighting and the details of planning and working, but here and now the critics are only trying to point out a better or surer or quicker way to win a victory which all foresee and for which all strive.

CONTRASTS WITH FORMER WARS

A glance at the history of America reveals that the unanimity of the present situation contrasts sharply with our past experience. There were many "loyalists" who opposed Washington and the War of the Revolution. Many thousands of them were refugees in Canada, and Valley Forge was not the only dark hour in those eight long years. It was even more serious in the war with England in 1812, for the opposition, present from the beginning, increased as the conflict went on. Massachusetts refused to respond to the call for troops at the outset, Connecticut would not allow the state troops to be commanded by United States officers, and the Hartford Convention, in 1814, threatened "direct and open resistance" to the national government. Nor was the next important war, that against Mexico in 1848, an exception. Prominent and influential men opposed the war openly and vigorously. It was on the occasion of seeing a recruiting officer enlisting soldiers for the war that James Russell Lowell wrote the dialect rhymes against the war in which occur the lines:

> As for war, I call it murder,
>   There you have it, plain and flat.
> I don't want to go no furder
>   Than my testament for that.

The War between the States was, of course, being a civil war, the occasion of much division and serious disunity. Opposition to the President was often bitter and outspoken, even in the North.

The war with Spain and that against the Philippines did not affect the country so profoundly, but there was opposition even then. When we come to the war of 1917, the story is the same, differing only in degree.

But in this present conflict the American people are of one mind in the determination to see it through to a conclusion favorable to our arms. And the citizen has a part to play—a more important part than in any previous war of modern times, for total war, in the present sense, is a new conception.

IMPORTANCE OF THE MIND

The point of view of social psychology is the one from which this discussion is presented. For war, which changes all things, changes the personality of all, and the psychological aspects are here considered of central, even transcendent, importance. The French school of warfare and strategy, of which Marshal Foch was one of the leading adherents, defines the very object of the activities of the army in psychological terms. The object of the commander of the armies—the goal of all strategy and tactics—according to this school, is not to kill the enemy or to destroy his property save as a means to an end, and that end is to destroy the enemy's will to fight. When this has been accomplished, the victory is won. When General Grant accepted the surrender of Lee, he issued rations to the rationless defeated army and sent the men home on their promise not to fight again, even permitting them to keep their horses, since "they will need them for the plowing." Psychological objectives having been attained, military action was no longer called for.

This recognition of the importance of mental influences is, thus, no mere academic theory. The propaganda efforts of all governments have assumed unprecedented proportions in this war. Our propaganda bureau is called the Office of War Information, and its staff numbers tens of thousands and its budget amounts to many millions. Bulletins, magazine articles, press releases, radio programs, movie films, and public addresses are sent out in a ceaseless and unbroken stream of words planned to influence the minds of men. This barrage of words is directed at the minds of the citizens at home and the allies across the seas, as well as at the few remaining neutral countries and, very importantly, at the civilians in the enemy lands. One speech was thus radioed 144 times in twenty-four hours. The minds of men are the target to be attacked by the bullets of phrases. To influence what people think and feel and believe is considered fully as important as to drive back a hostile army.

THE LOSS OF POWER

What are the changes that take place in the soul of the citizen when war fastens its grip on the land? One of the first is clearly the sense of a loss of power. In a democracy the citizen is assumed to be the source of all authority and power. The elected officials are chosen by him and are his servants, pledged to carry out the collective will. Some are chosen to high office but are rightly admonished to bear in mind that, though they have been raised above their fellow-citizens, they were raised by them. In a democracy the citizen is free; he can come and go at will, protected by his rights in the enjoyment of his home with his children around his table.

But with war comes a shrinkage of this autonomy. When my daughter bids goodbye to her fiancé who is off to the wars, when my youngest son leaves his school and his sweetheart to enter the Army, when another son leaves his young wife to fight beyond the seas, and when a fourth bids farewell to his little child and her brave but saddened mother, it is not hard to see that war changes all things. For war, of necessity, imposes limitations that are strange and new and hard. The whole way of life is altered from a regime of freedom to one of obedience. Regulations, orders, directives, and prohibitions limit progressively the accustomed autonomy.

Under the necessities of war the manufacturer is told what he can make, whom he may employ, and what wage he may pay and is punished if he pays either more or less than ordered. The merchant must learn from Washington whether or not he can buy goods enough to allow him to remain in business, and some of them are written off as war casualties. The farmer is directed what to produce, is limited as to his employed help, and has his prices regulated by a bureau and not by the market. Every citizen has his articles of consumption rationed, beginning with oil and gas, extending to sugar and coffee, and is reminded that more and severer regulations are yet to come. Added to this there is an increasing list of things that he cannot buy at all, beginning with automobiles, typewriters, and refrigerators and with many more such prohibitions expected before long.

All these the citizen accepts as necessary to win the war. If he grumbles it is not at the necessity for the restrictions, unless he is unconvinced as to some particular item in a long list. But most of the complaint is not against the restrictions as imposed but at the manner of their imposition, the way they are administered, and the mistakes of the administrators. If there is bungling or inefficiency or insolence or lack of consideration, the complaint may be loud and long—it may also bring improvement in the administration. But the citizen, at least the American citizen, knows the necessity of the restrictions and deprivations, and he accepts them with good grace, for he, too, wants to win the war.

ENLARGEMENT OF THE SELF

The feeling of the individual of helplessness, impotence, and unimportance due to the restrictions on his liberty and the almost complete disappearance of his rights is offset by an important change in his conception of the relation of his efforts to those of others. In normal times each goes his own way feeling at one with his own family, church, club, and the few dozen or hundred associates. Beyond these the bonds that unite him to the whole body of citizens are few or tenuous or nonexistent. But in wartime this, too, is changed. The assurance that his little efforts are merged with the work of millions gives worth and meaning to what he can do. His little contribution of rubber or scrap iron is indeed small, but there is a vision of hundreds of thousands of similar heaps that will swell the total, and his little self expands to unite with the population of the nation. This *esprit de corps* makes the separate individual citizen feel at one with his kind. Cherished plans may, indeed, be abandoned from necessity and the fondest hopes foregone, but the consciousness of the unity of the nation leads to a feeling of importance in being a useful part of the effort of a mighty people. The humblest task is ennobled and the slightest sacrifice is transformed if it is felt to be a contribution to the same work that occupies the time and strength of the President, the Congress, and the generals and admirals at the front. No other experience is comparable to war in producing this sense of solidarity and unity. If the tasks and sacrifices are taken in this spirit, well. If the individual is rebellious and disobeys the regulations for rationing gasoline, there is a fine of $10,000 or ten years in the penitentiary, or both. The laws in wartime do not rely on loyalty alone.

MUCH POWER REMAINS TO THE CITIZEN

But though the individual citizen feels himself shorn of his autonomy and bereft of his freedom and power, there is a limit to this deprivation. He may be ordered and directed, indeed, but in his collective expression he is respected and feared even by those who issue orders to him. Public opinion is not easy to measure, it is not easy even to define, but it is the source of power, the ultimate appeal, even in times of war. Not only in elections, when the protest vote can make even the most powerful rulers pause and force the resignation of administrators of vast authority, but even when not formally expressed or organized it is profoundly respected not only by the legislators who must think of re-election, but by all men in public life—ministers of state, appointed administrators, and generals of armies. No great decision is made without taking public opinion into account. Unorganized public sentiment in America is widely held to be the force that prevented the forcible occupation of the much-needed bases in Eire, and American opinion is destined to have an important influence in determining the fate of India. The ultimate source of all political power is, in the long run, the might of public opinion, in war no less than in peace. There are times when the individual citizen feels himself to be a small and unimportant cog in a vast machine, but the collective desires of the citizens when aroused and articulate resemble more the dynamo, without which the machine would not go. It is, of course, for this reason that the citizens of every nation in the whole world are the objects of ceaseless propaganda, for, however powerful the armies, the winning of the war depends on the success of the effort to win the minds of men. The loss of power of the citizen is not, therefore, without its compensations and limitations. Though much is taken, much remains—demos is still enthroned.

CHANGES IN HABITS

Of all the many changes that war brings, the alteration of habits is the most obvious. Adjustments are many at the very beginning of the conflict and become progressively more numerous week by week. These are too familiar to need much reciting here. Movements are curtailed by the shortage of rubber and gasoline, houses are altered in their internal arrangements to meet scarcity of fuel, eating habits are adjusted to diminishing supplies, and tin cans acquire an unexpected value. The empty room where the soldier son used to sleep and the vacant chair where he was wont to sit necessitate adjustment. The young wife with a husband in the service may move into another dwelling, and some of the little children of the soldier may go to live with grandparents. The ever increasing orders and restrictions force us out of the grooves of habit and compel new plans. Some find their incomes suddenly increased and become, collectively, a national problem; many find their incomes diminished or even discontinued and must go into new and unaccustomed activities. In short, no one in all the nation can continue to live just as he lived before. War changes all things, and habits are changed immediately. This is very important, but, important as are the changes in habits, they are less significant than the changes in the minds and hearts of men.

CHANGES IN THE IMAGINATION

It may well be contended that the images in men's minds are of more importance than the movements of their bodies, since, while they often are occasioned by those movements, they determine, in times of crisis, what the bodily actions shall be. Our conceptions of ourselves and of others are formed in the normal course of our experience, and these are in our minds as images. When a man rises to a new situation, he may have a revised conception of what manner of man he is, and this takes place as one of the results of war.

CONCEPTION OF ONE'S SELF

The good citizen plays multiple roles on the stage of his normal life in normal times. He goes about his business, earning his daily bread, pursuing his normal ambitions, and performing the part that falls to him in the family, the neighborhood, and the community. When the tocsin of war sounds and he finds himself doing what he can to forward the victory, there is a vital increment and a great change. Formerly seeking his own interests, he now sinks his private advantage and becomes a patriotic and devoted member of a great company. He no longer can seek his own private good, for it is not good to send a son to his death. He seeks the welfare of the whole, in the interest of which some men must be killed, even if it be his only son.

For he is now something that he had not been before, a comrade of those with whom he formerly had little in common. America was formerly a good land to live in, a land of opportunity, a land where the humblest could hope for advancement. America is now a nation struggling, perhaps in deadly peril; it is now his country. He is not one who is now seeking to advance or to better his condition; rather he is one who gives up gladly what he once held dear, and everything can be thrown on the altar—money, energy, resources, property, and even the life of his dearest.

This new self is an enlarged and exalted self. All those who are helping to further the war effort are his colleagues, his companions in a cause. The soldiers in the camp are his own people, and he is their supporter and loyal helper. He is a man who now is willing to go without butter that the soldiers may be well fed. The soldiers are his soldiers, "our men," and he feels at one with the forces in Africa, in India, and in the Coral Sea.

This enlargement of the self is the psychological aspect of the unity of a people and is a function of the state of morale in a people. When reverses come and the battle does not go well, especially if the enemy was, as so often happens, underestimated, there is always a measure of criticism of those who have the direction of matters, and a desire to replace the leaders who have failed in favor of others who are believed to be more able. Should the whole effort fail, the unity is completely disrupted, and the nation splits into violent factions, ready to attack and kill those who were formerly fighting on the same side. This is what happened in France, but only because France was defeated. It can be foretold of any defeated nation. In such a case, there is still another modification of the citizen's conception of himself.

It must be confessed that the unity of a nation is never absolute and that the sinking of the personality as far as private interests are concerned with the corresponding enlargement to include the whole nation as one's fellows is never wholly realized. The differences and divisions and conflicts of peacetime are softened, but they do not altogether disappear. Politicians still strive for office, and the "ins" try to stay in while the "outs" strive to get in. An electoral campaign in wartime can be very bitter with its charges and countercharges of inefficiency and of disloyalty. Such charges and accusations can leave painful wounds that will be long in the healing. Moreover, conflict groups and pressure groups may seize the opportunity to secure advantages that they had not gained in times of peace. Minority racial groups and organized economic federations may fight bitterly, even threatening dire consequences to gain their ends. There are envy and strife in unexpected places, and it is not strange that many look to hold in times of peace advantages that they could not have gained except for the war.

But this should be said. However selfish the groups may be, they all pay lip service to the cause of patriotism. Those blocs that are striving for their own advantage may, indeed, be selfish, but they speak the language of self-sacrifice and insist that to help them and to grant their demands is to help win the war. Those who oppose them may insist that the demands are ill-timed and a hindrance to the war effort. But both sides are alike in their professions of devotion to the cause of the nation as a whole.

CONCEPTIONS OF OTHERS

As there is no self without an other, the changes which war brings in the conception of one's self are accompanied by a corresponding change in the ideas of others. Now, important as it would be to know what the others really are, it is more important for human conduct to know what our conception of them is. As Holmes once wrote, when John and Tom meet, there are at least six persons present. There is the real John, known only to his Maker, there is John's idea of himself, there is Tom's idea of John—and, of course, three Toms. But there are really many more, and Cooley points out twelve—six on each side. For there is John's idea of Tom's idea of John, John's idea of Tom's idea of John's idea of Tom, and so on. Thus there are "echoes of echoes of personality" involved in the dealings of men with one another and also in the intercourse of nations.

Nor are these facts of little worth, for these images are so important as to determine the fate of armies and the destinies of nations. The solid facts of human life are, in very solemn truth, the facts of the imagination, as important as are the great tanks armored with steel and armed with heavy guns. If the point still seems forced, consider the realities of the American expedition to North Africa, a colony of France. Impressive as the physical preparations were, the expedition depended for its very existence on America's idea of France's idea of America's idea of France. That this idea might be accurate, daring visits were made by important emissaries whose task it was to ascertain what the French in North Africa were feeling and thinking. Why did the English attack on Dakar fail? Was it not because Britain's idea of France's idea of Britain was wide of the mark? The facts of the imagination are, indeed, solid facts.

The citizen's conception of others, and specifically of other nations, changes in wartime with the progress of events. The idea is a generalized undifferentiated one, sometimes called a stereotype—a metaphor from the printing trade. We speak and think of the English, the Chinese, the Italians, and the rest as if they were homogeneous, neglecting for convenience the many kinds of people who make up the vast populations. It is only when the future conduct of the government of a nation is in doubt that distinctions are made. China is China and Russia is Russia, but France is divided—the government at Vichy being opposed by another faction. Brazil is Brazil and Panama is Panama, but, when we think of Argentina, we tend to consider the different parties in the country, for, while the official governmental policy at the present writing is one of neutrality, pro-American sentiment is known to exist, and our government would like to get them into the war on our side.

Thus for purposes of wartime thinking we find the generalized idea quite adequate, although it is an obvious oversimplification. There are friends and there are enemies; there are neutrals whom we desire to remain neutral, such as Portugal, and neutrals whom we would like to enlist in the war. The one determining factor is the military alignment, and this may change. Russia, expelled from the League of Nations for her attack on Finland, was the object of bitter denunciation; attacked by Germany and fighting the enemy with whom we are at war, she becomes our ally. The British attacks against the French at Oran, in Syria, and in Madagascar were made against a former ally now turned into an opponent by the turn of events.

The determining factor in our conceptions of other nations is, then, their military alignment, not the form of government or the political organization or ideology. The word "democracies" was hardly accurate as descriptive of the allies, and the more accurate phrase "United Nations" has superseded it. Those who help us are our friends. What counts is the attitude toward the war.

THE EMOTIONS

The emotions of a man depend on the progress of the actions which he is performing or in which he participates by sympathetic observation or by vicariously imagining. During the progress of the war it is the news that has the determining influence on the emotions of the citizens at home. The defeat at Pearl Harbor occasioned surprise bordering on amazement, for the great fortress had been considered impregnable; anger at the enemy; sadness at the death of our men; and finally resentment against "someone" who was felt to be responsible, on account of the lack of foresight and alertness, for a disaster that should not have happened. Each message of triumph or disaster caused rejoicing or regret.

The news being the chief source of the emotions of the citizens, it is the task of the propaganda ministry, by whatever name it happens to be called, to present the news in such a manner as to control the feelings of the people in the interest of national morale. Because the enemy would surely profit from a complete reporting of the news if promptly published, a strict censorship is exercised over whatever is printed in the press or spoken over the air. There has always been a conflict between the reporters who want to tell the story of the battle and the censor who would prefer to confine the reports to laconic official announcements. A reporter who violates the instructions of the military is forbidden the status of a correspondent, as has happened in all countries and in every war. It is a difficult problem, and only compromise is possible. Bad news is depressing, but frankness in the publication of unpleasant tidings as promptly as possible, consistent with military security, is calculated to secure the confidence of the people. The penalty for concealment of unfavorable news is to be suspected of never being frank.

Besides the news, the governments of all countries issue floods of printed matter to influence the emotions of the people and to increase their confidence. Motion pictures are enlisted in the campaign, and the radio is now brought into the service of the war effort. The radio "technician" selects his material with the sole object of producing the emotions he desires. Mere accuracy is felt to be far less important than morale. One writer on radio in wartime has stated this matter with rare frankness:

> The technician of democratic propaganda must emotionalize the intrinsic truths to use them effectively. But in the execution of this task he can respect no single fact, no truth, so much that he will refuse to alter it if it does not fit into the total emotional pattern he is designing.[1]

There is, of course, nothing new about this except the frankness of the confession. Unfortunately, the method carries a penalty. It may succeed in producing the emotion, but, when the lack of respect for the truth becomes known and the alteration is discovered, loss of faith is sure to follow. One of the problems of the present situation is the result of just this method as it was employed in the first World War. There is much complaint among the propagandists of the present because the public is skeptical of atrocity stories. In 1916 they were believed. Then followed books like that of Philip Gibbs, *Now It Can Be Told*, and millions of people felt that they had been deceived, and resolved not to be taken in again, with the result that even the truth is often received with skepticism. It is dangerous not to respect the truth and serious to alter it deliberately.

As long as the war is going well, morale is not difficult to maintain, and the emotions of the citizens are easily kept at the optimum. When the end in view is long delayed, the emotions vary from confidence and assurance through hope and

---

[1] Sherman H. Dryer, *Radio in Wartime* (quoted in *New York Times Book Review*, December 13, 1942, p. 6).

anxiety to despondency and despair. When Waterloo was lost, the cry of "Sauve qui peut" rang through the scattered lines of the French. Failure in war is fatal to unity, and partial failure mars concord. If the general in command of a campaign is unsuccessful, he is often relieved of his command and another soldier is given his chance. The citizen is likewise critical and resentful of his leaders if the war effort is halting and there is suspicion of incompetence.

Critics like Mr. Willkie have spoken strong words on this point. Those in high authority are prone to resent criticism, but, when that is the case, it is time for the criticism to increase. Important changes in all countries have always been made in response to the aroused opposition and criticism of the public, and it is difficult to find any instance of an unwise change of this character where the criticism has been made by those who are loyal to the ends in view, however critical they may be of the means employed.

RUMORS

News produces emotions, but lack of news does not mean lack of emotion. The lack of news, where there is suspense, gives rise to rumors; and in the absence of information concerning a matter of keen interest rumors fly like snowflakes in a winter storm. Rumors are not individual phenomena but belong, like the folkways and the fashions, to the class of collective behavior. It is not impossible that some rumors are "planted" by enemy agents, but the number is surely negligible, and, even so, there is a favorable emotional soil or they would not be received or transmitted. Rumors imply hopes or fears or anxiety or, at least, curiosity. The propaganda ministry is always concerned about them, but there would seem to be no way of stopping them altogether.

Sometimes the facts are unobtainable and the interest great. When French Morocco was occupied, there was a period of anxious suspense concerning the location of the French fleet at Toulon. Rumors flew thick and fast. "It is on its way to Dakar." "It is on its way to Tunis." "It is on its way to join the Allies." "It is on its way to attack the British fleet." None of these guesses was true, and none was planted. When the President made an unannounced visit to the West, it was rumored that he was on his way to see Stalin, that he had come to settle a strike, that he had come to quiet a race riot, and more like these—all wrong. There was no news, hence the rumors. There is a dilemma which the office of censorship faces in dealing with rumors. It is impossible to publish all the news as soon as the public would like to hear it. Considerations of safety necessitate suppression. But suppression means rumors, and there is no help for it.

A scientific study of rumors has yet to be made adequately, but some competent men are now interesting themselves in the problem. Perhaps the most valuable result to be looked for in collecting rumors in wartime would be the index that might be furnished by the prevalence of the different types of rumors in the different parts of the country. It should be a useful method of learning about that powerful but elusive force—public sentiment.

THE IMAGE OF THE END-IN-VIEW

It is impossible to describe any deliberate act in physical terms alone. What a man is really doing is not known until his purpose is discovered. It is equally true of war. We are doing what? Fighting a war. But for what purpose? Unless this is clearly defined, not only will our action be without needed motivation, but the conclusion of the conflict will bring confusion and disorder. To say that we are fighting to escape slavery is mere rhetoric and negative rhetoric at that. General statements like the enunciation of Four Freedoms or the somewhat less vague words of the Atlantic Charter are still lacking in specific content and fail to satisfy the more thoughtful among us. Moreover, they are only the utterances of the heads of governments who may or may not be in office when the war ends.

In order that the carnage of war may not be all tragedy, there would seem to be need of some authoritative pronouncements by responsible representatives of governments that will formulate the common purposes in a way to produce the maximum effort now and to secure the greatest benefits afterward.

Is it possible to state in any such detail as the Wilson points what we desire to see accomplished? He spoke of Poland, of Italy, of Czechoslovakia, of Rumania. Are we to restore Latvia, Esthonia, and Lithuania? Is Java to be restored to the Dutch or Hong-Kong to the British? Some voices are insistently calling for a declaration on India. Some day we must answer all these questions and more. Can we answer them now?

The reluctance to raise these questions at the present time is easy to understand. Each of the fighting nations has its own ideas and its own interests. If debate on these details were opened at once, there would be controversy and a lamentable loss of unity and of the energy that should go into the war effort. Therefore, our leaders evade or postpone any declaration of the specific issues in the interest of present unity.

There is thus presented a real and serious dilemma. If we postpone peace discussions, there will be serious trouble after the war, and the issues may be settled by prolonged conflict. If we do not postpone the issue but try to formulate clearly what we are doing in this war, we run the risk of division and disunity. Certain it is that the diplomats will compromise as long as they can. The heads of the states are very greatly burdened with problems of administration. May it not be that the risk is too great?

It is the opinion of an increasing number of the thoughtful among us that, serious as the hazard is, it is desirable to undertake it and run the risk. When the war is over and our victory achieved, the settlement will be made by the strongest of the victorious powers. At that time there will not be the crying and imperative need for unity. All experience of peace settlements teaches us that the ideas of the victors are not easy to harmonize nor are their interests readily integrated. It will not be a simple matter to compose the interests and views of England, Russia, America, Australia, Greece, France, and the rest when all danger is past. A considered agreement, carefully worked out, would make the task of the treaty-makers lighter. It might even prevent another conflict, for historians know that the allies of today may be the enemies of tomorrow.

An increasing public sentiment favors the assumption by the citizen of this all-important responsibility. Already discussion is in progress in newspapers, in journals, and in thoughtful books urging the necessity of discussion and deliberation, with definite proposals thrown out to challenge consideration. In 1918 the task was left to a body of men, selected by the executive, and the results were highly disappointing. If our wisest and best citizens could, by discussion and deliberation, arrive at some defensible plan, and if this plan could have the approval of the Congress of the United States working in full harmony with the President and the Department of State, and if such a plan could be agreed upon in advance of the end of the war by the powerful governments of the world, the gain for humanity would be incalculable. But whether this desideratum is reached or whether the task is neglected, it remains true that it is the citizen who is the final ratifying authority. Public opinion is too powerful to be set aside for long; therefore, the responsibility of the citizen is great.

TREATMENT OF THE VANQUISHED

When the enemy lays down his arms in surrender, it will be the part of the victors to determine the fate of the conquered. History indeed records a few wars in which the settlement was conciliatory, but such instances are rare. We may be permitted to cite one.

The Boer War was fought fiercely for years, but, after the armies of the Dutch had been destroyed, the fighting kept on for a long time. It was necessary to gather into concentration camps all the women and children of the Boers, but even this did not bring peace. Finally a system of blockhouses and many miles of barbed wire induced the enemy to make a formal surrender. The peace was exceptional. It was a negotiated peace, stipulating that no one was to be held accountable for any acts of war. Not only was there no indemnity, the English actually gave $15,000,000 to their defeated enemies "to build the homes again." It turned out to be a wise peace, for in 1914, just twelve years after, England found herself in a greater war, and her Boer subjects fought side by side with their English conquerers.

It cannot be denied that, at the time these lines are written, the dominant note seems to favor very severe and even ruthless terms, once the war is won. Nor is it difficult for a sociologist to understand that men should so contend. The necessities of morale-builders lead them to represent the enemy in very bitter words. They come, as the war is prolonged, to be thought of as wholly and malignantly evil, referred to in the heat of oratory as being not men but predatory animals, and even racial theories are invoked to justify a Carthaginian peace. Ruthless severity is a natural reaction for those who believe that only in this way can the defeated be made conscious of their guilt and thus be brought to repentance.

ETHICS OF A RUTHLESS PEACE

But if the sociologist can understand why some want very severe terms, he can also comprehend why others oppose such a settlement on ethical grounds. There are those who insist that the concept of punishment is inapplicable to any post-war settlement on the ground that punishment can be assessed only by a disinterested and impartial arbitrator or judge, insisting that the passions of the victors who have lost so much ere the victory has been won will not make possible a fair and just settlement, that is, if punishment be the object. These advocates also argue that history often has reversed the judgment of the generation that fought. It is very rare, they insist, that historians are willing to assign the guilt of any past war to one side exclusively.

THE EFFECTS OF SEVERITY

The sociologist is compelled to note also that many thoughtful men question whether a ruthless peace does or can produce a sense of guilt. Moral judgments are notoriously relative. It is often impossible to judge one's own with the detachment of an impartial spectator. Men point to Nathan Hale, hanged as a spy by orders of a British officer, but honored as a hero by his own people, who erected monuments to his memory; and even to Captain Wirz of Andersonville prison, hanged for murder after the war was over but honored by a statue later on by the Daughters of the Confederacy. Repentance can be induced, but not every attempt to induce it is successful.

Everyone will agree that the peace should be a wise one. The question is how to find the path of wisdom. Is it possible to make a settlement that will commend itself to friend and foe alike? Is there danger that severity will lead only to self-justification? There are those who so believe. They point to Poland, obliterated politically for more than a century, having kept alive its national ambitions and the spirit of rebellion until the days of Wilson. They cite Bohemia's avenging the Battle of White Mountain three centuries after its defeat there, and to Latvia, overwhelmed in the thirteenth century but still aspiring seven hundred years later. Perhaps no one is wise enough to know the best way, but it is the citizen who, collectively, is the final arbitrator.

Our own domestic history provides an instructive case, for the War between the States was fought with great severity, and when it was over the South was treated with exceptional harshness that the conquered might come to repentance. For more than ten years armies of occupation remained in the South for what was euphemistically called "reconstruction." Unfortunately, the effect was the opposite of what had been intended. Southerners of each generation idealized the "lost cause," and the northern armies were represented to the children in the southern schools as invaders who came into the land to take away the liberties of the people.

Of the many literary expressions of the southern sentiment, we quote some stanzas from a poem by Father Ryan—verses that were recited in the schoolrooms of the South for many years and by thousands of children. It is called "The Conquered Banner" and reveals the temper of a defeated but unsubdued people:

> Furl that banner, for 'tis weary;
> Round its staff 'tis drooping dreary;
>   Furl it, fold it—it is best;
> For there's not a man to wave it,
> And there's not a sword to save it,
> And there's no one left to lave it
> In the blood which heroes gave it;
> And its foes now scorn and brave it;
>   Furl it, hide it—let it rest!
>
> .   .   .   .
>
> Furl that banner—furl it sadly;
> Once ten thousands hailed it gladly,
> And ten thousands wildly, madly,

Swore it should forever wave—
Swore that foeman's sword should never
Hearts like theirs entwined dissever,
And that flag should float forever
   O'er their freedom or their grave.

  . . . .

For though conquered, they adore it—
Love the cold dead hands that bore it!
Weep for those who fell before it!
Pardon those who trailed and tore it!
And, oh, wildly they deplore it,
   Now who furl and fold it so!

  . . . .

Furl that banner, softly, slowly;
Treat it gently—it is holy,
   For it droops above the dead.
Touch it not—unfold it never;
Let it droop there, furled forever—
   For its people's hopes are fled.

The mood induced by such writing—and there was much of the same kind—is, indeed, a feeling of romantic excess and despairing pessimism. It would have been wiser had the South proceeded to forget the past and made a new start at once. But the point of the argument of those who favor generous treatment of conquered enemies is that, human nature being as we know it, similar results are to be expected in analogous cases.

THE SOLID SOUTH

Not to dwell overmuch on the attitude of the South, it may be pointed out as a relevant fact that the "solid South" is a disadvantage, not only to that section but to the whole nation. It may, indeed, be true that the race question has been a very important factor in perpetuating the attitude, but even the handling of this delicate problem was not unrelated to the desire of the victors to punish the vanquished. Whatever the complexities of the situation are, and they are many, the fact remains that for eighty years the feeling of resentment has been strong and the feeling of repentance has been absent. Perhaps some students will not find the parallel instructive; others regard it as singularly relevant and as revealing the effects of a mistaken settlement.

While it is a great deal to expect that politicians will always keep in mind these considerations, political leaders cannot long resist a strong and articulate public opinion. The citizen in wartime? What more important consideration can claim his attention? When all is over, what will be America's idea of Germany's idea of America's idea of Germany—and similarly of Italy and Japan? On these solid facts of the imagination the fate of the world may hang. It is not the task of this writer to decide these things, but to us citizens, collectively, falls the responsibility to do what we can to prepare to shape the fate of the nations.

Whether there will be a magnanimous peace to be offered by a victorious coalition at the end of the struggle seems doubtful as these words are written, but the temper may change as discussion and argument proceed. The advocates of a vindictive or at least a punitive peace may prevail, and the sufferings that will have been undergone will, at least, make such a settlement understandable. What the thoughtful must weigh and consider is the possibility of a harvest of resentment and hate and revenge to be reaped, not in another twenty-five years this time, nor perhaps in fifty—but the memory of peoples is long.

We need discussion and information and understanding of the effects of the actions we contemplate. We are not to revile those who differ with us, whether they be of this party or that. Those who advocate ruthlessness are entitled to their opinion and should freely express it. Those who favor a generous peace must not be stigmatized as "appeasers" or pro-enemy or traitors to the cause for which we are fighting. Reason is not at home in the heat of passion; but any decision not based on reason will invite disaster.

But whatever the final decision—let it be tirelessly reiterated—the responsibility does rest on the intelligent citizen, whether he realizes it or not, whether he admits it or not, whether he shirks it or not. Thought and reflection, conference and deliberation, debate and discussion—these assume the dignity of duties in a time like this which has been called a time for greatness. If we make a great blunder, it will not be the first time that such a blunder has been made; if we find the best way, our children will rise up and call us blessed.

Our theme has been the role of the citizen in wartime. It now seems clear that the task of the citizen is as important as that of the soldier. The fighters are doing their part, but theirs is only a part. The sword can wound, but it cannot heal. Let no citizen yield to the fatalism of the multitude or feel powerless in time of war.

In times of peace there are some who clamor for war, but in times of war all men long for peace. The soldier will some day finish his work, and then the citizen will come fully into his own again. His power will be most wisely used if he is not caught unprepared for his responsible duties.

BIBLIOGRAPHY

The literature dealing with this subject is appearing in increasing quantity and continually. Every serious magazine has an article in almost every number.

The *American Journal of Sociology* has issued three outstanding special numbers which are noteworthy. They are: "War and Peace," Vol. XLVI, No. 4 (January, 1941); "National Morale," Vol. XLVII, No. 3 (November, 1941); and "Impact of War on American Life," Vol. XLVIII, No. 3 (November, 1942). The last of these (November, 1942) is a comprehensive survey, by twelve competent authorities, discussing all the important aspects of American life as affected by the war.

Some important books are:

COMMITTEE ON NATIONAL MORALE. *German Psychological Warfare.* New York, 1941.

The Committee on National Morale with headquarters in New York have made an extended study of German methods of propaganda and have learned much from them. They have issued several valuable publications in this field.

GILLESPIE, R. D. *Psychological Effects of War on Citizen and Soldier.* New York, 1942.

The title is self-explanatory.

HOOVER, HERBERT. *America's First Crusade.* New York, 1942.

This is a chapter of a book that was not to be published until after the death of the author. It was issued in 1942 because the "next war" occurred sooner than the author had expected. It presents the difficulties and disappointments that Wilson met at Versailles.

HOOVER, HERBERT, and GIBSON, HUGH. *Problems of a Lasting Peace.* New York, 1942.

This book lists the hindrances to a just peace and outlines a generalized plan to overcome the difficulties.

KEYNES, J. M. *The Economic Consequences of the Peace.* New York, 1919.

This well-known work was written to teach lessons from the last war but has no small value for this one.

THE JAPANESE-AMERICANS

ROBERT REDFIELD

❋

NINE months ago, and three months after Pearl Harbor, our federal government moved and confined about seventy thousand of our citizens against whom, individually, there was no showing of crime, misdemeanor, or disloyalty. These were the American-born children of Japanese parents. They were placed in confinement along with their enemy alien parents, and there most of them remain today.

The order of the President which authorized evacuation and exclusion of any persons from military areas was issued on February 19, 1942. During March, General John L. De Witt defined military areas in the Western Defense Command and ordered the evacuation by the Army of all persons of Japanese ancestry—about a hundred thousand of them—who had not removed themselves voluntarily from Military Area 1 and Military Area 2 in California. Events that have occurred since then include the following.

The Little Tokyos of the Pacific Coast disappeared, and ten new Japanese-American communities, held within bounds by armed guards, appeared in the mountain and middle western states. A well-known sculptor, a medical scientist of repute, some Los Angeles hoodlums, certain young leaders of American patriotic societies, older Japanese with outspoken loyalty to Japan, a family of mixed Japanese and American Indian parentage who had always thought of themselves as Indians, and, very probably, a few spies of the Japanese government—all found themselves living together in similar barracks and eating at common mess halls. A three-year-old child, who had lived among Caucasians, mistook the meaning of the strange faces about him and asked his mother why they had come to Japan. An American citizen with a Japanese father and an English mother pleaded guilty to evading the evacuation order and said he hated Japanese so much that he preferred to go to jail (with Caucasians) rather than to go to a relocation center with Japanese. As the country faced the first serious agricultural labor shortage, thousands of confined farmers and truck gardeners were kept from working. Certain state governors objected strongly to the admission of Japanese-Americans, as confined evacuees, to their states and not much later took steps to bring them in to harvest sugar beets or pick cotton. The War Department suspended admission to the Army of Japanese-Americans; nevertheless, Americans of Japanese parentage were reported fighting the Japanese in New Guinea, and a movie audience in a midwestern city applauded a film showing maneuvers by an all-Japanese-American military unit in a camp in Wisconsin. One of these soldiers, on leave, returned to California to visit Caucasian friends and was arrested (and released) for violating the order excluding such as he from the Pacific Coast. He said he did not mind; his leave was up anyway. A veteran of World War I, with an excellent military record, killed himself when faced with the evacuation order. A civilian organization, co-operating with agencies of the federal government, tried hard to place Japanese-American students, released from the relocation centers, in colleges and universities in the country, and local chapters of the American Legion tried hard to prevent it. Universities found themselves invited by one branch of the government to accept such released students and warned by another branch that to do so might be to fail in protecting military contracts. The Attorney-General of the United States ordered that Italian aliens in this country be no longer treated as enemy aliens; meanwhile American citizens of Japanese parentage remained in confinement. Italian citizens got back their short-wave radios and cameras; Americans of Japanese parentage got a new program providing for certain kinds of conditional releases from relocation centers. A western patriotic organization memorialized representatives of government for a constitutional amendment to cancel the citizenship of all persons of Japanese origin in this country. The American Civil Liberties Union got busy, and Norman Thomas wrote a pamphlet.

Only about one hundred thousand people were directly affected by the evacuation order. The Japanese-Americans constitute less than one-tenth of 1 per cent of our population. In a series of lectures dealing with the effects of the war upon the United States, justification for including a lecture on the effects of the war on the Japanese-Americans is not to be found in the effects upon this small ethnic minority, although it is true that to no other ethnic group inside our nation has war brought greater changes. The justification for talking about the impact of war on the Japanese-Americans lies rather in consideration of what has happened or may happen to all the rest of us as a result of the evacuation and confinement of the Japanese-Americans and in the larger issues which the smaller problem illustrates.

The scattered reports I have just cited indicate that Japanese-Americans have been put in a position which might be described as ambiguous. These reports indicate also that, as regards the attitude taken toward the Japanese-Americans, the American people are, to say the least, confused. There is no clear and common attitude with regard to them. In a time of war, when the nation feels the need for a new solidarity and to a great degree achieves it, the Japanese-Americans are looked upon with every shade of favorable and unfavorable feeling. There are some who regard them as the unfortunate victims of one of the milder forms of mass lynching. At the other extreme is the Californian who asserted that all the Japanese in our country should be taken out to sea and sunk there. In between are perhaps a majority of our countrymen who think that the Japanese problem here was solved by the evacuation from the Pacific Coast, and who think no more about it.

THE PROBLEMS OF DIVIDED LOYALTY

The confusion may be explained by the fact that in the Japanese-Americans we have most acutely presented the double problem of divided loyalty. The problem is double in that it may be considered from the point of view of the ethnic minority itself and also from the point of view of the American people as a whole. Every immigrant group has the problem of divided loyalty: the belonging to the country of origin and the belonging to the country of adoption. The past belongs to one nation or race; the future belongs to another. The immigrants and their children must make the transition, and the passage involves conflict within the group and struggle within the individual personality. The experience of the immigrant is the experience of all America, where everyone is an immigrant; and the problems of the passage from the Old World to the New—a passage at once geographical, cultural, and psychological—have been abundantly recorded in fiction, autobiography, poetry, and scientific report. The Japanese-American is but one of the many more or less hyphenated Americans who have gone to make up our nation.

But he today presents the common problem in a sharpened form. In the first place, he is one of the relatively few kinds of foreigners to whom we have denied the opportunity to become a naturalized citizen. Therefore, although he sees his son born an American, he must himself forever be an alien. In the second place—perhaps this fact should come first—his racial type marks him off from the Caucasian majority. The label of his difference from us is there to read. It is there equally to misread in the case of Americans of Japanese parentage who have been born and reared in our country and have become Americans inside while remaining Orientals outside. In the next place the Japanese-Americans find themselves identified with the enemies of the United States. They find themselves regarded not merely as aliens of another race but as enemy aliens of another race. And, finally, the fact of confinement in the fenced communities called "relocation centers" has enormously intensified the problems of an ethnic minority in transition. For now those who think of themselves as Americans and those who think of themselves as Japanese and those who have not known just how to think of themselves have been thrown together to face a common depprivation of privilege and liberty. Outside these centers, before the war, a family of Japanese origin that had become a part of America, sharing the general ideals, could live among Caucasians, or could at least, by mere physical avoidance, escape the acuter forms of conflict within the community. Now Japanese grandfathers are living in the same room with their American sons and telling their entirely American grandsons things that the middle generation would not have said to its children. Now, in each relocation center, there is one enforced society of people who are all treated the same way and who must work and play and act together with an intimacy and common responsibility that goes far beyond what was true in the Little Tokyos of California. Now the old people, who are Japanese, can and do say to the young people who are Americans, "What good is it to you to be an American? If you are an American citizen, and it matters to be an American and an American citizen, why do you not walk out into America past that armed sentry at the gate?" Before the war there was a fair chance for the American born of Japanese father and mother to make his way into American life. Now he is thrown back upon his Japanese forebears, and he doubts if passage into American life will ever open for him again.

The divided loyalty which the situation of the Japanese-Americans presents to the Caucasian citizen of the nation is of another sort. On the one hand, there is the loyalty to our country as a leading representative of the principle of equal opportunity for all men. Even now, in time of war, we take new pride in consciousness of the fact that this land was built by minority groups. In our very racial and cultural differences we find a base for our country's unity. A Chicago newspaper, seeking no doubt to contribute to this sense of solidarity, publishes a series of articles on the contributions of groups of alien origins to American life. In a song which quickly became popular the many ethnic sources of our country are pridefully sung:

> Am I an American? . . . . I'm just an Irish, Negro, Jewish, Italian, French and English, Spanish, Russian, Chinese, Polish, Scotch, Hungarian, Litvak, Swedish, Finnish, Canadian, Greek and Turk and Czech and double Czech American. . . . .

At the same time the country begins to realize that it is and must be a member of a world community of nations. Wendell Willkie is not the only American to discover that the cause of China is the cause of the United States and that Iran and India and the United States, as well as England and the United States, have common problems and responsibilities. Within our own nation the Negroes ask for a treatment somewhat nearer fairness than they have had in the past, and the temper of the country, stirred with this new sense of the mutual needs of ethnically different groups, is on the whole disposed to advance toward meeting the demands. From this point of view the Japanese-Americans, as one kind of American, call for the loyalty of America.

Nevertheless, the "Ballad for Americans" does not mention the Japanese. We do not feel them to be part of us as we feel the Czechs, the Poles, the Italians, and, indeed, the Germans to be part of us. From the point of view of that loyalty which war makes, it would be disloyal to include the Japanese-Americans. For, in a way which Italians and Germans do not represent, the Japanese are our enemies. They are the enemy with whom, in the first months of the war, we met in closest and bitterest combat. The pain we suffered at Pearl Harbor and on Bataan turns again within us when we see a face or hear a name that stands for our Japanese enemies. We distinguish Nazis from Germans. Not all Italians are followers of Mussolini. We know these things and recognize them. But the Japanese are all "Japs." The Japanese, in the thinking of most of our people, are all one thing: a people fanatically devoted to the destruction of the United States—our enemies, all of them. The loyalty of war will not allow tender feeling toward anyone felt to be a representative of the Asiatic enemy. A Caucasian employed in one of the War Relocation centers as manager of the garage and superintendent of the Japanese-American automobile mechanics, a mild and pleasant father of a family, resigned his position after trying for several months to make a go of it. "It's no use," he said. "I just can't be happy with them. I just can't think of them except as Japanese." He meant, of course, as Japanese on the other side of the lines at Guadalcanal. Yet his mechanics were boys born and reared in Oakland and Pasadena and Salt Lake City.

THE EVACUATION FROM THE WEST COAST

The remoter consequences of the evacuation—the really significant and far-reaching consequences—were not clearly in the minds of anyone when the evacuation was ordered. The reasons for the evacuation were immediate reasons. They were summed up in the phrase "military necessity." We shall probably never know whether the evacuation was required by military necessity. At the time the justification was little questioned. It is today probably generally held to have been necessary. But doubts have arisen which were not there before. Then we saw a danger of invasion of the coast by Japanese forces. The danger is not so great now, and perhaps it was not so great then as we thought. Then it was pointed out that the concentration of Japanese populations in areas of military importance and the control by Japanese or Japanese-Americans of land adjoining military objectives made a situation favorable to the commission of sabotage. Today we look back on nine months in which little or no sabotage of Japanese origin has occurred in the United States, or when at least little or none has been reported to us. We see now that in Hawaii, where inhabitants of Japanese origin form a much larger proportionate part of the population, there was no evacuation and no segregation; and yet in that still more crucial outpost of our defenses no significant Japanese sabotage is known to have occurred. (Very recently there has been a suggestion that some of the Hawaiian Japanese may be evacuated.) In the light of the present we can see that when we ordered the evacuation of the hundred thousand we must have been badly shocked by the treachery of the Japanese at Pearl Harbor. There must have been, security or no security, a disposition to defend ourselves against enemies or supposed enemies that were near at hand. Or was it, perhaps, to revenge ourselves? To what extent was the act we performed a wise act in the national interest and to what extent was it a gesture expressive of our alarms and our aroused anger? It is easier now than it was then to remember the anti-oriental feeling that has smoldered or flamed in our western states, to recall the tradition of the vigilante, and to see that there were economic interests in California and elsewhere that stood to gain by the expulsion of the Japanese. It will be a profound historian who will make a sure and just judgment on the matter in later years.

At the time of evacuation the controversy was not whether the evacuation should take place but whether time and other practical considerations allowed for an examination of individual cases before their evacuation, so that only individuals against whom some showing of possible dangerousness would be evacuated. The arguments made showed that some of the probable results of indiscriminate evacuation were foreseen by some people. Especially was it asked if it would be constitutional to remove citizens indiscriminately. But in spite of doubts on this point, and of arguments in favor of selective evacuation, indiscriminate evacuation, which could be quickly accomplished, took place. The Army removed the hundred thousand within 137 days of the first removal. Meanwhile a civilian agency of government, the War Relocation Authority, was established to "relocate" the evacuated people from the temporary assembly centers to places in the United States away from the seaboards. As it seemed clearly unwise to dump a hundred thousand dispossessed enemy aliens and their citizen children, against whom strong feeling was running, into communities which would on the whole refuse to accept them, the new Authority established the ten new Japanese-American communities in California, Idaho, Wyoming, Montana, Utah, Colorado, Arizona, and Arkansas. Today all of the evacuees have been moved for the second time from the temporary assembly centers established on race tracks or in fair grounds and settled, as compulsory colonists, in the ten strange new towns.

THE RELOCATION CENTERS

Nothing quite like these communities has ever appeared before in the history of America. The relocation center suggests an Army camp, for the Army built the centers, and the inhabitants live in Army barracks arranged in the stark regularity that is usual in Army camps. The relocation center suggests an Indian reservation, for its denizens are a racial group that has been moved, in some such manner as the Cherokee were once moved, and that has been forced to live within narrow limits. The inhabitants, racially distinct, are led and administered by a largely Caucasian staff; indeed, not a few of these staff members have been drawn from our Indian Service, and one entire community, at Poston, Arizona, is directly administered by the Indian Service. The relocation centers suggest also the resettlement projects of our Department of Agriculture: there are the usual problems of getting agriculture going and of setting up all the institutions which a good-sized town requires. And, finally, these strange communities inevitably suggest internment camps. Indeed, if to confine behind wire fences patrolled by soldiers a population chosen for confinement solely for military or political reasons is to set up an internment camp, then these relocation centers are in fact internment camps.

Yet to declare that they are, without saying more, is to make a far too simple statement. There are other camps, about which the public is told less, in which enemy aliens who are known, individually, to be dangerous, are much more strictly confined and watched. The relocation centers are conceived of as places where this minority is to make a new start in American life. Some of the inhabitants regard their deprivation of liberty as a sacrifice required of them, as Americans, for the public good. Others go to war; they go to relocation centers. It has been suggested that the situation compares with that in which a number of Typhoid Marys are believed to be present, but unidentified, in a large population; until the individuals that actually carry the contagion can be identified, all the population must be put in a sort of indefinite quarantine.

Moreover, looked at as internment camps, these relocation centers belie all comparison with Dachau and Oranienburg.

This is, you say, a strikingly un-American thing we have done: to confine tens of thousands of our fellow-citizens against whom, individually, no charge is made? Very well, it is a strikingly un-American thing we have done. It may be added that we have done it in a strikingly American way. For within certain broad limits the evacuees are to make their own government, institutions, and social life as they want to make them. The official statement of policy of the War Relocation Authority declares:

It will be up to them [the evacuees] to plan the design of their community within the broad basic policies determined by the Authority for over-all administration of such Centers. They will establish and manage their own community government, electing their own officials. It will be largely up to them to maintain a community police force, a fire-fighting force, recreational facilities, and many other essentials.

And this is what, in general, is happening. The officers of the Authority try earnestly to put responsibility for making and for carrying out decisions upon the evacuees. The chiefs of the principal administrative sections of each center assemble around themselves assistants drawn from the evacuees. Policies are discussed with the Japanese-Americans. The hospitals are staffed by doctors and nurses many of whom are of Japanese origin; the official who makes the important decisions as to what room in what barracks an evacuee family is to live may be an evacuee himself. The chief police officer is, in more cases than not, a Japanese-American. The Board of Judicial Review, which is in this period of organization in effect a criminal court trying petty offenses, is, in the case best known to me, composed of a majority of evacuees and a minority of Caucasian staff members. The forms of government are emphatically democratic. In each center a special officer is responsible for local government; he explains and supervises the many elections that take place within the center. The visitor to the center is struck with the great number of assemblies; people seem to be meeting constantly to discuss some measure or to vote on some issue or simply to divert themselves. There are meetings to elect block representatives, to discuss the plans for the co-operative store, to choose a queen of beauty, to organize the fire department, to worship—Buddhists as well as Christians have their places of worship—or to enjoy an evening of amateur entertainment. And the evacuees who have been drawn from states with absentee voting laws are encouraged to vote by mail in their home elections.

Nevertheless, the paradox remains: this democratic, more or less American way of life is being built up behind bars among a people who are, on the whole, not trusted by the rest of America. The evacuee who is urged to exercise a right of franchise is not allowed to leave the center except under conditions of extraordinary personal necessity (or under the terms of a release program which I shall speak of later), and in many cases he must go in the company of a Caucasian. The Board of Legal Review hears cases without suggestion of arbitrary power. Yet it is well known that the director of the center exercises delegated authority from the war power which would probably allow him to take almost any action he might reasonably think to be in the public interest. And behind all the activity, behind all the meetings and discussions and voting and persuasion by sympathetic Caucasian staff members of evacuees to take the burdens of responsibility upon themselves —behind all this lies the uncertainty as to the future. No activity, however fair-minded and democratic within the camp, can carry full conviction to men and women who do not know whether their future is to be that of free and accepted members of the wider American society.

It would not, then, fairly represent the curious societies which are developing in these new Japanese-American settlements to compare the evacuees with internees and the Caucasian staff with wardens or guards. The policy and practice are one of collective effort to build a new community. The quality of the Caucasian staff is probably more than ordinarily high, and it certainly includes men and women with devotion to liberal and humanitarian ideals. But circumstances make it impossible for the people of the center to become one big happy family. After all, the Caucasians have the authority and the liberty; the evacuees have been confined by coercion. The evacuees are being fed and housed and even clothed at the government expense and are provided this minimum of subsistence whether they choose to work or not. So they are cheaply fed, and housed in barracks, one family to a room. But the Caucasian staff must be provided with a standard of living sufficient to attract them into the employment, and therefore they eat superior food in a dining-room of their own, and at some centers where building materials have been available they may rent attractive little apartments in the centers. The Caucasian staff member may send his children to the schools that are now established in the centers, or he may send them outside the centers to schools in near-by towns. These differentials of opportunity and choice develop lines of stress within the new society. A visitor may form an impression of an idealistic leadership struggling bravely against present circumstances as well as against a tradition of anti-oriental feeling.

CONFLICT BETWEEN THE GENERATIONS

The possible serious results to our country from the evacuation of the Japanese include some consequences which are near at hand and others which are more remote. An immediate possible consequence is the loss to us of the loyalty and support of many Americans now in the centers. It may first be asked if indeed they are loyal. A distinction must be made among three principal groups. Of the Issei, those born in Japan and in most cases also reared there, a military intelligence officer who has studied the matter for many years thinks that the large majority are at least passively loyal to the United States. On the other hand, there are certainly not a few who wish strongly a Japanese victory and who are contemptuous of the United States. It is to be remembered that the denial of right to become American citizens has no doubt affected some of these. In the second place, there are the Nisei, those born and educated in this country. The average age of this group is about twenty-two; they constitute almost two-thirds of the total Japanese-American population; as time goes on they will, of course, form a larger and larger part of it. These are the young men and women who are, on the whole, Americans and whom we may hope to keep in our way of life. A very large majority of this group are probably loyal to the United States. Their Americanization has proceeded far in our schools and in our communities. A third group, the Kibei, those born in the United States but educated in Japan, constitute the most difficult problem, for among these are some who are strongly pro-Japanese and no doubt a few who have been planted here by Japan; but also among them are individuals who reacted violently against the militarism of modern Japan and returned to this country strongly loyal to the United States. Within the Kibei group, and between Kibei and Nisei, there are not infrequent dissension and conflict.

The first problem is to save the loyal, especially the many young Americans, for America. Before the war there were difficulties: the denial of citizenship rights to the parents of these young people; the anti-alien land laws, the racial prejudice. Nisei were not always sure which government stood behind them, that of Japan or that of the United States. Until 1924 the Japanese government regarded persons of Japanese parentage born in this country as citizens of Japan. (It should be mentioned that many sought to free themselves from this identification even before the practice ended.) The older generation were organized into an association with the financial and moral support of Japan. Nevertheless, I repeat, the young people, born and brought up in this country, were, by and large, Americans, loyal to this country.

But now, in the relocation centers, the pressure from their Japanese parents and grandparents is stronger than ever. The strength of the Japanese family organization, the youth of the Nisei, and, above all, the undeniable fact that neither loyalty to America nor the enjoyment of citizenship rights has made any difference in the treatment accorded the evacuees—these circumstances have put the young Nisei in a weak position. If the Nisei assert their loyalty to the United States vigorously and openly, they promote discord within the family and they are met with the remark I have already quoted: "If it matters to be an American, why don't you walk out of that gate past the sentry?" If the Nisei compromise with the pro-Japanese, they must listen to pro-Japanese utterances and must make their own loyalty appear doubtful.

The Caucasian leaders of the centers are caught in the same dilemma. The immediate task is to organize a community; to this end solidarity and harmony are needful. But the larger objective is to keep the Nisei for America, and to do this it would seem necessary to treat them as Americans and to treat them more favorably than the disloyal. Early in the history of the enterprise a compromise decision was made which illustrates the problem. It was decided that only Nisei, the American-born, could hold elective offices in the community, but that the Issei, the Japanese-born, could vote in the elections. The decision has not been easily accepted; Nisei as well as Issei have been troubled by it, feeling it hardly proper that the children should hold the offices while the fathers stand aside, and fearing an increase of conflict within the family. Yet if the Authority had allowed the older people to hold the elective offices, the communities might have been controlled by the smaller Japanese element. These communities must be democracies, we have said, but they may not be pro-Japanese democracies.

The dilemma cannot be solved so long as both loyal and disloyal, citizens and aliens, are confined together and treated similarly. Many have therefore applauded a development of policy and program by which evacuees may leave the centers. They may leave them temporarily for certain purposes, or permanently to accept employment anywhere in the United States outside of the military zones on the Pacific Coast. A placement program, promoted by the War Relocation Authority and co-operating civilian organizations, is going forward. Several hundred evacuees have left the centers and have found employment in industry, offices, or homes, and several hundred more students have been released from the centers and have been admitted to colleges and universities. It is chiefly the Nisei, the American born and bred, who have been released under this program, although the way is open to Issei and Kibei as well. It is only those against whom the Federal Bureau of Investigation has no evidence of disloyalty, and of these again it is only those who are shown to be welcome in the places where they are to go. The number affected is yet small relative to the numbers in confinement. But the program offers the hope of incorporation of young Japanese-Americans into our society. The colonization of the evacuees in the relocation centers substituted a new segregation, a ghetto-like segregation, for the Little Tokyos that existed before the war; but the new program tends to disperse the Japanese-Americans throughout our country.

THE EFFECTS UPON AMERICAN ATTITUDES

But will our country accept such a dispersion? Are the Japanese-Americans wanted as full members of the American community? To ask this question is to point again to the spectacle of Americans torn between the loyalty to the cultural and racial pluralism within our unity and the principles of fair play which are involved, on the one hand, and the conception of the Japanese as our enemies, on the other. If the Japanese-Americans are not, in person, our enemies, they seem to represent our enemies so that we cannot accept them as our fellows. We never treated them fully as our fellows before the war. Now, in the emphasis of in-group and out-group which the war brings about, they are thrust out still further by those who see them as the untrustworthy, the disloyal, the hostile. Those who see them so see them not in the light of their own knowledge of individual Japanese-Americans but in terms of preconceptions as to nationality and race and as guided by limited conceptions of patriotism. So, while many church groups are striving to bring about the acceptance of released evacuees into American communities, the Sixth District of the American Legion votes to urge the federal government to keep all persons of Japanese parentage locked up during the war and to deport them to Japan when the war is over; and the Native Sons of the Golden West are reported as raising funds to support action designed to bring about cancellation of the citizenship rights of Americans of Japanese ancestry.

This last-mentioned report is worth pausing over. An organized group of our fellow-citizens is asking that another group of our fellow-citizens, distinguished solely by their descent from persons of a certain race, be deprived of their citizenship rights. This time this is being advocated not in Nazi Germany but in California, U.S.A.

Shall we disregard the reported action of the Native Sons of the Golden West as irresponsible and not likely to accomplish its purpose? Before we do so we might wonder if the evacuation and the confinement already accomplished have not provided some foundation for such possible excesses of repressive action. It is doubtful if any deprivation of civil rights so sweeping and categoric as this has ever been performed under the war power and justified by our courts. The constitutionality of the recent measures has, of course, been challenged in legal actions. Several of these are on their way through the courts, and at least two have resulted in findings, in inferior courts, that the evacuation was constitutional. The question may be dismissed with the cynicism that the Supreme Court always waits until the war is over to tell us that an action found necessary during the war was unconstitutional. Perhaps so. The present case will offer unusual difficulties to counsel supporting the constitutionality of the measures taken. When it is argued that the evacuation was necessary because of the danger of sabotage by members of the Japanese community, it will be asked why it was not found necessary to evacuate Japanese-Americans from Hawaii. When it is argued that these people had to be evacuated for their own protection from a fearful and angry Caucasian population, it will be asked if the government is establishing a principle of "protective custody" of suspiciously foreign flavor and offensive to the Bill of Rights. And if it is conceded that the evacuation from the endangered Pacific Coast was constitutional, it will yet be asked with what justification are citizens confined in camps in Arkansas without any hearing?

As a result of the actions taken, the Japanese-Americans have suffered losses of property and of liberty. Worse than that, they have suffered a loss in security in the sense that they are not sure where their children are to live and prosper. They have lost the vision of their future.

Nevertheless, the consequences of the measures taken are greater than these and concern all of us. We have moved and held in confinement citizens selected for this treatment by reason of their racial origin. In doing so, we have stigmatized the bearers of these racial marks as untrustworthy. To the advocate of yet more repressive measures the action already taken by the government seems a justification for further steps. A speaker for a local American Legion post supported his plea that young Americans of Japanese parentage be not admitted as students to a middle western college with the argument that the government had locked up what he called "the Japanese" for the duration and that therefore the college was disloyal in its position and the Legion was loyal in trying to prevent the admission of the boys and girls of Japanese parentage to the college and its community. A people already set apart by prejudice and discriminatory legislation has now been further set apart.

For the center of the present problem, and the seed of the future consequences for America, lies in the fact that the evacuation and the confinement were done on a racial basis. It was not the disloyal who were moved and established in relocation centers. It was not the enemy aliens who were moved. It was both the loyal and the disloyal, the aliens and our fellow-citizens, who were together so treated. It is difficult to escape the conclusion reached by the military authority I have already mentioned. Writing in the October, 1942, issue of *Harper's* magazine, he said: "The entire Japanese problem has been magnified out of its true proportion, largely because of the physical characteristics of the people." Most Americans cannot look at the Oriental as they look on the Caucasian. It was right to confine the Japanese-Americans, it was declared. It would have been wrong to confine Americans of German parentage. The Japanese-American, it is felt, by those who do not know him, is somehow harder to understand and is probably more dangerous.

The consequences lie outside of our country. They lie in the effects of what we have done on the conduct of the war and on the making of a world after the war. Now we need, and then we shall need, the help and confidence of Asiatic peoples. The wholesale evacuation of persons of Japanese origin cannot

but be explained in Asia as another evidence of racial prejudice. It is now being so explained by Axis propagandists.
This explanation of the action is feared and the action de-
plored by more than one Chinese in this country. Moreover,
the racial explanation appears to the American already preju-
diced as a justification, governmentally pronounced, of his
prejudices. The Japanese-American evacuation and confinement are eloquently dissonant with what our liberal leaders say
today about China and India.

Whether we shall keep the young Americans with Asiatic
faces for our way of life, and whether we shall prevent the unfavorable effects just mentioned upon our relations with Asiatic peoples, will depend in large part on the success of the
program whereby Japanese-Americans are released to become
students or to take jobs in the towns and villages of the United
States. For it is not true that the government has ordered the
confinement of the evacuees for the duration. It has restricted
their freedom pending a real relocation in American life. That
relocation is now going on. It is the policy of the War Relocation Authority, the agency of government charged with this
task, to encourage the release of the Americans of Japanese
parentage who are not known to be disloyal. If a larger and
larger number of these young people can be placed in employment and in education throughout the country, and if they are
welcomed there and return the welcome with the hard work
and orderly behavior which have always strikingly characterized them, the problems raised by the evacuation will be in
large part met. The evacuees still in the centers will see a good
future before them and will take heart to become fully Americans. And our enemies will find it less easy to say that we do
not trust Asiatics because racially they are Asiatics.

Whether the relocation program into American communities will succeed depends chiefly upon the people of those
communities. In some communities today the evacuees are

welcome; in others they are unwelcome; in many there is a conflict between those who welcome them and those who do not. The conflict, I repeat, is the conflict of the two loyalties—seeing the Japanese-American as a crucial case for the testing of the fairness and justice implied in the American ideal versus seeing the Japanese-American as a representative of our enemy in the war. Each of us has a part in the resolution of that conflict.

BIBLIOGRAPHY

ANONYMOUS. "The Japanese in America: The Problem and the Solution," *Harper's*, October, 1942. (By an intelligence officer.)

BALDWIN, R. "Japanese Americans and the Law," *Asia*, September, 1942.

BIDDLE, F. "Biddle Reveals Plans To Intern Japanese," *China Weekly Review*, November 22, 1941.

BROWN, ROBERT L. "Manzanar—Relocation Center," *Common Ground*, autumn, 1942.

CLARK, BLAKE. "The Japanese in Hawaii," *New Republic*, September 14, 1942.

"Evacuation of Enemy Aliens from West Coast Areas," *Interpreter Releases*, March 4, 1942, and April 9, 1942.

Exploratory Study of West Coast Reactions to Japanese. Washington: Office of Facts and Figures, 1942.

FISHER, GALEN M. "Japanese Evacuation from the Pacific Coast," *Far Eastern Survey*, June 29, 1942. (Discussion of causes and effects.)

HOUSE SUBCOMMITTEE ON APPROPRIATIONS. "Statement of M. S. Eisenhower, Director of War Relocation Authority; Leland Barrows, Executive Officer, W.R.A.; and Colonel Karl R. Bendetsen, Assistant Chief of Staff, Fourth Army and Western Defense Command," in *Hearings on First Supplemental National Defense Appropriation Bill for 1943* (77th Cong., 2d sess.), Part 1. Washington: Government Printing Office, 1942.

LaVIOLETTE, FORREST E. "The American-born Japanese and the World Crisis," *Canadian Journal of Economics and Political Science*, November, 1941.

LaViolette, Forrest E. "Types of Adjustment of American-born Japanese." Unpublished doctor's thesis, University of Chicago, 1938.

McWilliams, Carey. "Moving the West-Coast Japanese," *Harper's*, September, 1942.

Miyamoto, Shotaro Frank. "Immigrants and Citizens of Japanese Origin," *Annals of the American Academy of Political and Social Science*, September, 1942.

———. *Social Solidarity among the Japanese in Seattle*. "Publications in the Social Sciences," Vol. XI, No. 2. Seattle: University of Washington, 1939.

Thomas, Norman. *Democracy and Japanese Americans*. New York: Post War World Council, 1942.

Tolan, John H. (chairman). *Findings and Recommendations on Evacuation of Enemy Aliens and Others from Prohibited Military Zones, May, 1942*. Report 2124 (77th Cong., 2d sess). Washington: Government Printing Office, 1942.

———. *Problems of Evacuation of Enemy Aliens and Others from Prohibited Military Zones:* Parts 29–31: *February 21–March 12, 1942*. (77th Cong., 2d sess.). Washington: Government Printing Office, 1942.

RACIAL IDEOLOGIES

ROBERT E. PARK

✹

PUBLIC OPINION AND REVOLUTION

SOME months ago—August 16, 1942, to be exact—the *New York Times*, commenting on the anniversary of the Atlantic Charter, pointed out that the tragic events of the preceding twelve months had served as a commentary on and an interpretation of that historic document, making its words and phrases seem, as the writer put it, more significant and more acceptable in 1942 than they had been in 1941.

The experience to which the *Times* editorial refers is one which most of us have doubtless shared. Great changes have taken place and more are impending. In the course of an incredibly brief space things that were once familiar have begun to look strange and eventualities that seemed remote are now visibly close at hand. We are all of us, it seems, in somewhat the situation of the expectant traveler, who, as he approaches his destination in some new and strange country, sees the dim and visionary outlines of a distant landscape slowly rise above the horizon and assume, in the measure that he approaches it, the form and substance of an actual world. At the same time, as a result of the rapidity with which events have moved, the world in which we have lived is, it appears, visibly receding. Nevertheless, we are still far from our destination, and the shape of things to come is still obscure.

Far-reaching changes are taking place in every aspect of social life, economic, political, and cultural, owing directly to advances in science and technology but indirectly to the urgent demands of a world war. The war has given unprecedented impetus—to cite a single instance— to invention and discovery in the field of chemistry, and this has brought about in turn something like a renaissance in all related sciences. So rapid have been the advances that, as one writer puts it, "already our world of 1940 is so distant in the past that it has become an antiquity, as seen through scientific eyes."[1]

Some of the revolutionary changes taking place, however, are in men's minds. Here are some of them as described in the *Times* editorial to which I have referred:

The concept of nationality is being limited by universal necessity.

We no longer believe that small nations can be sovereign or that the sovereignty of large nations can include the right to expand by force.

We realize that freedom of commerce is not a negative thing, the result of noninterference, but a positive result of international effort.

We begin to understand that peace is not possible without some supernational agency capable of making economic, political, and military decisions.

This world war is also a world revolution. . . . . The word "revolution" need not alarm the timid. . . . . It can be a revolution not of destruction but of reconstruction.

I have quoted the *Times* on war and revolution, not because I am, at the moment, interested in specific statements of editorial opinion or creed but because these particular comments on the current scene seem to indicate the direction and the progress of the nation's adjustment to the national emergency and to be an index of changes in the public mind more fundamental than those registered from day to day by the Gallup poll in its effort to keep the public informed in regard to public opinion and national morale.

[1] Dr. Charles M. A. Stine, in an address before the general session of the American Chemical Society, Buffalo, N.Y., September 7, 1942, entitled "Molders of a Better Destiny" (*Science*, October 2, 1942).

Changes in public opinion are, in the strict sense of that term, never revolutionary, because, for one thing, public opinion is concerned with what is in process and therefore problematic and debatable. Public opinion is the public mind in unstable equilibrium. The changes to which the *Times* refers, on the other hand, as far as they are indices of anything that could properly be described as revolutionary, are changes not so much in opinion as in orientation and point of view. They seem to reflect changes that have arisen in the public mind not in response to something in prospect but in response to *faits accomplis*. They indicate, perhaps, the efforts of the public mind to keep up with events and to achieve what one may describe, in the language of W. I. Thomas, as a new "definition of the situation" and a new point of view.

Differences of "definition," in the sense in which Thomas uses that term, are differences in the folkways and mores. As these differences are not ordinarily or obviously the product of discussion, they are not ordinarily discussible. To say that folkways are not debatable and hence nonrational, is, however, no more than to say that they are matters of custom and common sense. Possessing them, we respond to familiar situations with much the same spontaneity and unreflecting assurance that we would if folkways were instincts. This spontaneity and assurance with which we perform familiar and customary acts are, nevertheless, sometimes quite mistaken. Anyone who has witnessed the fanatical devotion with which a setting hen will sit on a glass egg will realize that, with all the assurance and conviction a hen may display, she is sometimes terribly and pathetically wrong. The fact is that neither instincts, folkways, or common sense—all of which are characteristically nonrational—can be trusted outside the situations and the habitats to which they are adapted.

If folkways are nonrational, there is, nevertheless, some wisdom or, as Sumner put it, some philosophy implicit in them. Thus custom, when interpreted by the courts, tends to assume the character of a principle or rule of law. In much the same way the will and the wisdom, implicit in the customs of peoples, emerge from the conflicts and controversies which more intimate association of races, peoples, and cultural groups provokes. They emerge in the form of creeds, doctrines, or, to use a term that has suddenly acquired a new and wide currency in the United States, ideologies.

IDEOLOGIES AND THE HISTORICAL PROCESS

What students of society and politics know about ideologies and about revolutions seems to have its source, for the most part, in the literature inspired by Karl Marx and by the writers who inherited the Marxian tradition. Darwin had described the historical process by which the manifold types of animal life were evolved as a struggle for existence in the course of which the earlier and less competent individuals and species were superseded by later and fitter forms. Marx seems to have adopted the Darwinian thesis, but with important qualifications as far as it applied to man, under the conditions imposed by human society. In the case of human beings the historical process, as he conceived it, has ceased to be a struggle of individuals and of species for existence in a purely natural economy, such as exists among plants and animals living together in a common habitat. It has become rather a struggle of economic or functional classes for social status in a social hierarchy.

The situation is not essentially different, as far as I can see, if the conflict is racial rather than economic, the classes, in that case, being castes and the dominant group a majority instead of a minority. In fact, racial conflicts where they occur are perhaps more elementary and logically, if not historically, earlier in the historical sequence.[2] In any case, the point is

---

[2] "The Nature of Race Relations," in *Race Relations and the Race Problem*, ed. Edgar T. Thompson (Durham, N.C.: Duke University Press, 1939), pp. 43–45.

that the conflict of classes, or of races, in becoming forensic and political, ceases to be a mere clash of blind, brute force and assumes a form and character that Herr Hitler has described as "spiritual," that is, a kind of psychic warfare in which the weapons are words, slogans, so-called "vital lies" and other forms of propaganda, not excluding the news and the editors' and columnists' interpretations of it.

Ultimately, however, the historical process, as Marx conceives it, tends to assume the character of a prolonged Socratic dialogue or discussion, in the course of which not only a new, more inclusive, and presumably more tenable point of view emerges but a new social order. The new point of view and the assumptions on which it is based constitute in that case the logical structure of the new social order. The process, which is at once social and logical, Marx, using the language of Hegel and Plato, called "dialectic."

Revolutions and ideologies seem to be a characteristic of modern or at any rate of civic life. They arose historically, with the decline of tribal societies and the rise of cities. Among the things we miss in primitive society is anything that corresponds with what we ordinarily understand by either public opinion, ideology, or revolution. Organized public discussion and public opinion seem to have first come into existence when the market place was converted into a public forum. It was, apparently, in these forums that men's beliefs began to assume the form of creeds, and the myths which grew up to support traditional beliefs assumed under these circumstances a rational and an ideological character.

Actually the way in which a new society and a new social order grows up within the shell of the old is not, even as Marx conceived it, as simple and intelligible a process as this summary statement suggests. The point is, however, that social change and social revolution, under human conditions, always involve not only competition but conflict; not always the clash of physical forces, as in the case of wars or strikes, but of the ideas and of the ideologies by which the contending forces are inspired and directed. Thus every war tends to become an ideological conflict, i.e., tends to become a revolution.

THE SOCIOLOGY OF KNOWLEDGE AND THE "COLLECTIVE MIND"

Recently a new school of sociological thought, if not a new science—the sociology of knowledge—has risen above the intellectual horizon of Europe. Seeing in the current social myths and in the "collective dreams," as well as more rational forms of knowledge which emerge in the course of social revolutions, a significant social phenomenon, it has undertaken to study empirically the function of ideologies and utopias in the evolutionary process.[3] Thus the sociology of knowledge turns out to be a study of the nature of the collective mind, provided one means by "mind," either in the individual or in the group, what historians mean when they refer to "the mind of an age" or "the mind of an epoch," namely, the mental patterns, traditional ways of thinking, including the memories, mores, and, in general, the common sense which men in any society ordinarily employ in judging the value of objects, the importance of actions, and the credibility of current interpretations of events. In short, a mind is the instrument with which men think; and, according to the sociologists of knowledge, this instrument is very largely, if not wholly, a social and socialized product.[4] This is necessarily true, since we think with what we know, and knowledge is science only when it is verified and verifiable.

Collective thinking, where it goes on at all, invariably takes the form of a dialectic process or discussion in which in-

[3] Karl Mannheim, "Utopia," *Encyclopaedia of the Social Sciences*, XV, 200–203.

[4] Robert Redfield, *Tepoztlán: A Mexican Village* (Chicago: University of Chicago Press, 1930), pp. 222–23. Also Henry Osborn Taylor, *The Medieval Mind* (5th ed., 1938); and James Harvey Robinson, *The Making of the Modern Mind* (New York, 1923).

dividuals and groups, having different interests and different points of view, seek to achieve some sort of understanding and some sort of agreement or at least some statement of their differences that is consistent and intelligible. What we ordinarily describe as public opinion arises where the issues are political and pragmatic rather than theoretic and ideological. One of the conditions of any sort of public opinion is the existence of (1) a public and a forum where criticism is tolerated and of (2) what is called in academic parlance a "universe of discourse," that is, a fund of fundamental ideas and assumptions which are understood and taken for granted but not, under ordinary circumstances, debatable. It is within the limits of such a universe of discourse that the discussions out of which public opinion emerges ordinarily take place. When, as often happens, in the course of a discussion, participants find they are not in the same universe of discourse, the discreet thing to do is undoubtedly to permit the discussion to subside before it reaches an embarrassing impasse. If it is to continue without violence either in word or in deed, an understanding may perhaps be reached by redefining the terms, making explicit the assumptions upon which differing points of view rest. But this is a kind of game which is not easy for experts and is practically impossible for ordinary human beings and politicians, that is, people who have real interests at stake. Political debates are fruitful when they are confined to discussing the means by which ends are to be achieved rather than ideologies by which ends are justified and legitimatized.

As a matter of fact, fundamental points of view and the assumptions on which they are based do not ordinarily get into public discussion either in the societies or communities where they are, so to speak, indigenous and generally accepted or in the societies and communities in which, in the light of generally accepted notions, they are likely to appear quaint, irrational, and generally unintelligible. Discussion, like other forms of communication, goes on easily and amiably when it is not concerned with fundamentals. Nonetheless, the fundamental assumptions continue to influence attitudes and get, in obscure, sublimated, and symbolic forms, some sort of overt expression, even where they are not discussed and not discussable.

The case of the Negro is an instance. Those who know the Negro spirituals will readily recognize in them the expression of the messianic hopes of the Negro slaves, and anyone who has heard Negro voices sing "Go down, Moses, way down in Egypt's land, tell old Pharaoh let my people go" cannot mistake the import of that hymn. Now that Negroes are free and have become race, if not class, conscious, they are in a position to state their case in more articulate fashion. However, the authors of the Declaration of Independence and the United States Constitution have provided them with a ready-made ideology.

Obviously much goes on in the collective mind that is not articulate and cannot be construed in the form of a dialogue or conversation. There is always in every culture and every society what William Graham Sumner called a "strain for consistency"—a consistency that is effectively achieved, perhaps, only in primitive communities but that is not altogether lacking in more complex and more sophisticated societies. This strain for consistency, which goes on ordinarily below the level of clear thinking, tends to impose uniformities on the meanings and mentalities of peoples and classes even in those instances where interests are so divergent that discussion of them in parliament, press, public forum, or anywhere that public opinion is ordinarily formed, is difficult or impossible.

For example, there is invariably a tendency within a public, parliamentary, or other discussion group to polarize opinions and form parties to support them. When that tendency persists to the point of creating within a public or a parliament irreconcilable and intransigent blocs, then discussion may be said to cease and war begins.

Conflicting and fundamental points of view are likely, however, to remain, if not suppressed, at least submerged, as long as the conventions are maintained intact and social routine not greatly interrupted. They force themselves into public consciousness and demand recognition, however, in time of crisis. In such case, anything that tends to heighten the tension makes communication, even for the purposes of ordinary intercourse, difficult, and public discussion, as a means of clarifying issues, ceases to function.

In such a case, the difficulty is not that people have differences of opinion about specific issues but rather that they look at things from fundamentally different points of view. Points of view give perspective to our thinking, and when they are defined by doctrines and assume the character of ideologies, they insure (1) consistency in the collective acts of societies, sects, and social classes and (2) integrity to the life-policies of the individuals who compose them. This seems, in fact, to be the peculiar function of ideologies.

It is characteristic of men that, when they undertake to act consistently and on principle, they measurably lose their capacity to respond to events in terms of equity and mere common sense. There is, as I recall, a rule of law that declares it is more important that the law be consistent than that it be just. I can see why this should be true. We must know what to expect of our laws, and we cannot do so unless courts are consistent. This explains, I suspect, the fact that the strategy of labor, in its disputes with capital, has been to appeal to public opinion by picketing or by strikes rather than submit its dispute to arbitration or to the adjudication of the courts. Public opinion is more likely than law to decide issues on the merits of the individual case. A court of arbitration inevitably interprets issues in accordance with tradition and recognized principle. The principle is conceived retrospectively in terms of an order, that is. The strikers, on the other hand, view the case prospectively in terms of what they hope for.

The whole point of this discussion, I might say, is based on the difference between public opinion and law, ideology or doctrine.

RACE RELATIONS AND RACIAL IDEOLOGIES

Much has been happening to race relations in the South in the course of the present war. They are not so cordial as they were. In the movement and changes which the national emergency has occasioned, the racial structure of society seems to be cracking, and a *modus vivendi* that survived the Civil War seems to be under attack at a time and under conditions when it is particularly difficult to defend it.

But great changes in race relations, mostly for the better, have been going on over a considerable period in recent years. These changes have come about in response to (1) improvement in Negro education and education generally in the southern states; (2) the rise of a responsible and conservative Negro middle class; (3) Negro migration from the rural South to the industrial cities of the North; (4) a marked decrease if not in interracial homicide at least in mob violence;[5] and (5) the rise of a Negro intelligentsia able to state the case of the Negro to Negroes in an increasingly influential Negro press and to the world at large in a growing body of literature which is always interesting, sometimes eloquent, and often disturbing in its revelations.

As a result of these changes it has seemed that the status of the Negro in the North, if not in the South, had been approximating that of other racial and cultural minority groups.

---

[5] Lynch law is no longer tolerated in the southern states as it once was. Opposition to the institution, if one may so describe it, in becoming active in the South, has ceased to be sectional.

Nevertheless, racial ideology and the point of view from which people in the South and in the North look at race relations seem to have changed but little if at all, and the conflict that is going on today in the South seems to be the expression of the determined efforts of southern white people of all classes to maintain at any cost the traditional racial etiquette and the traditional symbols which reflect the traditional racial structure of southern society.

Some twenty-eight years ago Thomas Pearce Bailey, in a volume entitled *Race Orthodoxy in the South*, made a statement of the racial creed and the racial doctrines of the southern people. The accuracy and authenticity of that statement, as far as I know, have never been questioned. This statement was neither an attack nor a defense. It was rather an exposition and explanation in the course of which the author expressed the conviction that, whatever else one might say about the racial doctrines of the southern people, they are inexorable historical facts and probably represent the only terms upon which the two races can continue to live together. Racial attitudes, according to Bailey, are, I might add, not instinctive but traditional. They are, in the South, at least, a part of the religious culture. Here are the items of this creed:

1. "Blood will tell."
2. The white race must dominate.
3. The Teutonic peoples stand for race purity.
4. The Negro is inferior and will remain so.
5. "This is a white man's country."
6. No social equality.
7. No political equality.
8. In matters of civil rights and legal adjustments give the white man, as opposed to the colored man, the benefit of the doubt; and under no circumstances interfere with the prestige of the white race.
9. In educational policy let the Negro have the crumbs that fall from the white man's table.

10. Let there be such industrial education of the Negro as will best fit him to serve the white man.

11. Only Southerners understand the Negro question.

12. Let the South settle the Negro question.

13. The status of peasantry is all the Negro may hope for, if the races are to live together in peace.

14. Let the lowest white man count for more than the highest Negro.

15. The above statements indicate the leadings of Providence.[6]

What Bailey has described as racial orthodoxy in the South is merely a more vigorous local expression of the racial ideology of the United States as a whole. It can all be summed up in one or, at most, two pregnant phrases: "This is a white man's country." "The Negro is all right in his place."

The first phrase, though it was coined in the South and is rarely heard in the North, seems to me to characterize pretty fairly America's attitude North and South, East and West, toward colored peoples, including the Indians, particularly when they came to this country from Mexico. The second phrase applies only to Negroes and characterizes the peculiar attitude of the southern white population toward the Negro. The difference is that in the South the Negroes have a place, if only they would stay in it; in the North, as far as there is any racial doctrine that could be described as orthodox, the Negro, the Indian, and the Asiatic have no place at all. They are merely more or less tolerated aliens.

The racial doctrines with which we are familiar in the United States are obviously the product of the controversies provoked by the racial problem. While the attitudes of the American people North and South, East and West, differ in emphasis and in detail, they are, it seems to me, fundamentally the same. Back of these racial doctrines is the whole history

[6] Thomas Pearce Bailey, *Race Orthodoxy in the South* (New York: Neale Publishing Co., 1914), p. 93.

of the South and of the United States. One is able to record and read these racial creeds, but it is impossible to understand them unless one knows intimately the people in whose minds they grew up. For racial ideologies are no mere logical artifacts, formulas, or general conceptions; they are rather the historical products of long-continued conflict and controversy.

The southern people have been obsessed with this problem of race relations all their lives. It has been a source of a lively interest and anxiety for three hundred years. Needless to say, it has been during this time a concern of Negroes also. The whole history of the United States, North and South, has forced upon Negroes in slavery and in freedom a race consciousness that has slowly created out of individual men and women without history and without traditions a people conscious of common destiny; in short, a self-conscious minority with a cause and an ideal if not an ideology.

It is obvious that a doctrine and ideology that is deeply rooted in the geography, the economy, and the intimate personal relations and etiquette of the races of the South is not something to be swept away by anything short of war or revolution. As a matter of fact, the Civil War and the revolution that accompanied it in the period of reconstruction did not change, fundamentally and at once, the relations of races in the South or elsewhere.

Nevertheless, changes have taken and are taking place. These changes began when the freedmen first realized that they were free to change masters, so to speak, and to move from one plantation to the next. It changed profoundly when Negroes began to leave the plantation altogether and make their home in the slums of the cities, where they had a freedom that exists nowhere else except on the frontiers of settlement and civilization. It has continued to change with the progress of Negro education in the South and with the migration of the Negro population to the North, where they have in the public schools the same opportunities to get an education as the immigrant and all the other national and racial groups of which the American population is made up.

The most profound changes in race relations, if not in racial ideology, have come about with the rise of a hierarchy of occupational classes within the limits of the Negro race, so that Negroes can and do rise to some sort of occupational and professional equality with other races and peoples who have not been handicapped by the segregations and institutions of a caste system. The class system, as it exists in the United States at least, does permit individuals and eventually races to rise. At present, at least in the northern cities, to which the Negroes in recent years have migrated in such large numbers, the status of the Negro population is no longer that of a caste. It is rather that of a racial and cultural minority; like the Jews, the Japanese, and, perhaps, the Indian and Mexican.

RACE RELATIONS AND NATIONAL SOLIDARITY

Owing, no doubt, to regional diversities of the country and of the peoples who settled it, the United States has always had the problem of maintaining national solidarity. In the early days of the Republic this problem took the form of sectionalism. Sectionalism, and the divergence of interests and ideologies that grew up as a result of these regional differences, rather than differences in national or racial origins, was responsible for the Civil War. Since that time, with the advent of the so-called new immigration from more distant countries and culturally diverse peoples, and particularly with the emergence of the Negroes as one of America's national and racial minorities, the problem of national solidarity has assumed a new and increasing importance. At the present time, although there is little or no immigration and the different races and peoples of which our population is made up have been pretty thoroughly distributed and culturally assimilated, they still cherish, nevertheless, their ancestral traditions and still look with nostalgic interest to the lands and the peoples from which they and their ancestors sprung. The world wars, in which America has been involved, have inevitably intensified this consciousness of kind and have tended to make the United States less a federation of territorial than of racial and cultural units. This sense of difference is maintained by the fact that peoples of the same racial stock, even when they marry in their class, marry nevertheless in their own racial and national group, so that the United States tends to become a congeries of racial and national groups. The problem of national solidarity today is not one of sectionalism but one of racialism.

Meanwhile, with the progress of the war, the issues involved are becoming clarified, and the points of view of the contending parties, the Axis and the Allies, are obviously in process of redefinition. The war, which began as a struggle for living space between the "haves" and the "have-nots," has become a struggle between the master-races and the rest of the world; the former to gain the political and cultural hegemony of the world, and the latter to achieve a new social order that will insure at least a measure of freedom, independence, and security to individuals and peoples, irrespective of race, such as they have not hitherto enjoyed. In short, the issues which were economic and political have become racial and cultural.

The entrance of the United States into World War II has given the American public a new orientation and a new issue. With American soldiers fighting on every front in every part of the world, the political and cultural horizon of the American people has suddenly expanded and become like the war—global. Americans are now, more than ever before, finding themselves living not merely in America but in the world. Under the conditions which this war has imposed, isolation as a geographical and geopolitical fact has ceased to exist and isolationism as a doctrine and policy has become obsolete.

All this has resulted in sudden if not profound changes in our attitudes toward those peoples, white and colored, with whom we are now allied and with those others all over the world whose fate seems somehow bound up with our own. We have hitherto maintained toward the peoples of India, China, Japan, and Africa a curious attitude of complacency verging on contempt. Toward peoples of a different color we have usually acted as a benevolent "master-race," possessing all the wisdom and therefore entitled to impose our political and religious institutions and social practices upon both lands and peoples.

But now that we find ourselves fighting on the same battlefields for the same cause, all this seems to be an anachronism. Faith in a democratic social order which asserts that all men are or should be brothers rather than masters and servants is more contagious when men find themselves fighting together in a life-and-death struggle for a common cause. Under these circumstances we have begun to conceive of ourselves as possibly living on terms of neighborly intimacy and mutual understanding hitherto undreamed of with peoples all over the world. This is the good-neighbor policy, as we have learned to interpret it, since we have come to think of the peoples of South America as allies rather than as customers. But it is inevitable that the good-neighbor policy must eventually extend to all the peoples with whom we are now allied and whose cooperation we must have in winning the war and carrying into operation the terms of the peace. The good-neighbor policy involves, apparently, not merely an alliance of governments but an understanding of peoples.

Under these circumstances many people in the United States have become suddenly conscious of the limited and parochial view which our previous isolation has fostered and are now apparently in a way to revise their opinions of alien peoples and to improve, at least, our international and interracial manners.

Few Americans are as yet prepared to go as far as Lawrence K. Frank would have them. In a recent number of *Free World*, under the title, "World Order and Cultural Diversity," he has stated the racial issues of the present war in a way which reveals, to be sure, their international importance but makes our responsibility for them almost personal and moral rather than collective and political merely. "What Hitler, with his assertion of a German master race has done," he says, "is to reveal, in all its stark ruthlessness and self-centered, almost paranoid, distortion, what Western European culture has accepted as the major premise of its international relations."

In spite of the new orientation and the sudden awakening which the war has brought about, it has not, thus far at least, profoundly changed the mind and the mentality with which the American people look at this matter of race. In the nature of things it could not. There is too much race consciousness to permit it. There are still relatively few people in the United States who are able, even if they wished to do so, to treat a Negro democratically, that is, on his merits as an individual rather than as a representative of his race. This is where the racial policy of the Anglo-Saxon American differs from the racial policy of Latin America. This is likewise the point at which people of the United States cease to be intelligible to the people of Brazil.[7] On the other hand, it is just here that the racial policy of the United States is identical with that of Australia and South Africa, whose racial ideologies must be reckoned with in winning the war and making the peace. And then there is India, Mother India, with her mélange of unassimilated races and peoples! Should India decide, at the conclusion of the war, to participate in organizing the peace,

[7] Donald Pierson, *Negroes in Brazil* (Chicago: University of Chicago Press, 1942).

how will she reconcile her caste system at home with democracy abroad?

It seems obvious, to an increasing number of people in the United States, that the ability of the United Nations to win the peace will depend upon their ability to achieve a new, profoundly different, perhaps one might describe it as revolutionary, change in their attitudes toward alien and particularly colored and colonial peoples.

It is obvious, however, that ideologies, since they are basic, since they reflect the point of view from which we look at the world and the point of view from which we interpret events as they occur, do not and cannot change with every change in opinion and every wind of doctrine. It is these ideologies rather than public opinion that represent the public mind, as far as the public can be said to have a mind. They are rooted in the memories, the tradition, and the mores of the particular community or society in which each of us lives; they reflect the mentality and habits of thought with which any society and the individuals who compose it determine not only what is right or wrong but what things we hear—rumor, propaganda, or news—are credible. Things that happen, which from the customary point of view are quite unconscionable, cannot be reported even in a press as free as we have in America and could not be discussed if they were.

I might add that, with all its recent realism, and in spite of the success that propaganda experts have had in measuring opinion, in improving or undermining morale, it seems doubtful whether political science has thus far discovered any technical devices capable of bringing about changes in the public mind that can properly be described as revolutionary. Revolutions are the product not of changes in opinion but of changes in ideology and in those common understandings and assumptions which make differences of opinion communicable and public discussion possible.

What the war has done thus far has been to make race relations an international rather than a local and national problem. We may expect, therefore, no matter how great the changes the war brings, that racial and cultural conflicts will continue in some form or other in the future as in the past. Nevertheless, the issues of the world war and the world peace will be very largely determined by the progress and outcome of this ideological conflict.

Furthermore, in the prosecution of the war and in the organization of the peace, racial diversities of the American population will be either a national handicap or a national asset, depending upon our ability to make our racial policies and our racial ideology conform to our national interests. We have not succeeded in doing that yet. A revolution in race relations in the United States may be impending, but it has not yet arrived. The war has changed the nature of the race problem, but it has not changed fundamentally the mind of the American people.

I can bring this discussion to no better conclusion than by quoting the words of Winston Churchill's latest broadcast. "It is not much use pursuing these speculations further at this time, for no one can possibly know what the state of Europe or the world will be when the Nazi and Fascist tyrannies are finally broken."

One thing, however, seems certain: the races and peoples which fate has brought together in America and within the limits of the larger world economy will continue, in the emerging world society, their struggle for a political and a racial equality that was denied them in the world that is passing. As far as this prediction turns out to be true, it will be, perhaps, because the historical process, as it operates among human beings, is determined finally not merely by biological but by ideological forces, and not by what men have or are merely but what they hope for and believe.

BIBLIOGRAPHY

BAILEY, THOMAS PEARCE. *Race Orthodoxy in the South*. New York, 1914.

COPELAND, LEWIS C. "The Negro as a Contrast Conception," in *Race Relations and the Race Problem*, ed. Edgar T. Thompson. Durham, N.C., 1939.

———. "Racial Ideologies and the War." (Unpublished.)

DOMAN, NICHOLAS. *The Coming Age of World Control*. New York, 1942.

ENGELS, FRIEDRICH. *Die Entwicklung des Sozialismus von der Utopie zur Wissenschaft*. 4th ed. Berlin, 1891. Translated by E. AVELING, London, 1892.

GRAEBER, ISACQUE, and BRITT, STEUART HENDERSON, *et al. Jews in a Gentile World: The Problem of Anti-Semitism*. New York, 1942.

HOOK, SIDNEY. *Reason, Social Myths, and Democracy*. New York. 1940.

———. "Materialism," *Encyclopaedia of the Social Sciences*, X, 209–20.

JOHNSON, CHARLES S. *Patterns of Negro Segregation*, chap. x, "The Ideology of the Color Line." New York, 1942.

MANNHEIM, KARL. "Utopia," *Encyclopaedia of the Social Sciences*, XV, 200–203.

———. *Ideology and Utopia*. New York, 1936.

MARCUSE, HERBERT. *Reason and Revolution*. Oxford, 1941.

MEAD, GEORGE H. *Mind, Self, and Society*. Chicago, 1937.

SIMAR, THÉOPHILE. *The Race Myth*. New York, 1925.

THOMPSON, EDGAR T. (ed.). *Race Relations and the Race Problem*, chap. i, "The Nature of Race Relations," by Robert E. Park. Durham, N.C., 1939.

VOEGELIN, ERICH. *Die Rassenidee in der Geistesgeschichte*. Berlin, 1933.

WRIGHT, QUINCY (ed.). *Public Opinion and World-Politics*. Chicago, 1933.

CRIME

EDWIN H. SUTHERLAND

✿

THIS analysis of the effects of wars on criminal behavior is made with three questions in mind: First, do convictions for crimes in general, for the several types of crimes and for the several classes of the population, increase or decrease in wartime? Second, what do the statistics of convictions mean in terms of the behavior of people? Third, what specific or abstract elements in wars produce the changes in criminal behavior and in convictions?

TRENDS IN CONVICTIONS

The facts regarding changes in crime rates in wartime cannot be determined with accuracy. Criminal statistics, which are always inadequate, become grossly inadequate in wartime because of new war laws; because of changes in administrative policies and personnel, in the composition and geographical distribution of the population, in the substitution of administrative boards and military tribunals for civilian criminal courts, and in national boundaries; and because of elimination of many items from the statistical reports. It has been necessary to rely for criminal statistics principally on the reports of England, Germany, and Austria during the first World War. This is unfortunate because it prevents adequate comparisons of modern totalitarian wars with earlier wars of a different type. The conclusions derived from these statistical reports and from nonstatistical descriptions of behavior in wartime are presented as nine factual generalizations.

1. *Convictions of all classes.*—The absolute number of convictions in civilian courts decreased in all the nations in all the wars for which statistical data are available except Canada in the first World War, where an increase of 4 per cent was reported with no allowance for the withdrawal of hundreds of thousands of men for military service. The decreases in the absolute number of convictions in many countries were as much as 30–40 per cent.

2. *Convictions of males.*—The absolute number of convictions of men decreased in countries at war. This is due, obviously, in part to the mobilization, by which millions of men, at the age when the conviction rate is usually highest, were withdrawn from the competence of the criminal courts. The problem is: Did the withdrawal of a large number of young men from civilian life result in as large a decrease in convictions of men in civilian courts as should be expected from the pre-war rate of convictions of men of those ages? A precise answer to this question is impossible because of inadequate statistics of the age distribution of the military force at a particular time and of the age distribution of the persons convicted in a particular period. A rough calculation, in which little confidence should be placed, was made by using English statistics, which were the best available; this resulted in the conclusion that a reduction of 20 per cent in convictions of men in civilian courts should have been expected and that the actual reduction was only 10 per cent. This means that men who remained in civilian life had an increased rate of convictions. The convictions of soldiers before military tribunals in the war period were approximately 33 per cent less than the convictions per thousand men of the same age before the civilian courts in the pre-war period. This finding is in conflict with the conclusions of several studies made about seventy-five years earlier, which referred to soldiers who were hired to fight or who were committed to the army instead of to prison. In England in the first

World War the number of convictions of men in civilian and military courts combined was less in the average war year than in the average pre-war year.

3. *Convictions of women and children.*—The number of convictions of juveniles and women increased in wartime. I shall present the evidence regarding the trend in juvenile delinquency in some detail because of the current interest in this topic. Mr. J. Edgar Hoover stated in a lecture in October, 1942, that juvenile delinquency is increasing in the United States with great rapidity. A juvenile court judge in New York City said, "There seems to be a crime wave among young boys here." Several other authorities have made similar statements. The evidence, although not uniform or entirely convincing, points in that direction. Several cities have reported increases in the juvenile delinquency cases, and a smaller number have reported decreases. Several state institutions for juvenile delinquents have reported increases in the number of admissions, and a smaller number have reported decreases. These statistical reports are not entirely convincing because great and indeterminate changes have occurred in the composition of the population in many of the communities reporting on delinquency rates, the time elapsed since the beginning of the war has been short, and the number of communities from which reports have come is small and perhaps selected in a biased manner.

The evidence as to what happened to juveniles in the United States in the first World War is no more uniform. The Children's Bureau reported that the number of juvenile delinquency petitions was larger in 1917–18 than in 1915–16 in six cities, smaller in two, and approximately the same in two. In a few other scattered communities for which reports were made the trends in juvenile delinquency cases varied similarly. That is the full extent of the evidence.

England is the only country from which reports as to the

trend in juvenile delinquency in the present war have become available. The absolute number of juvenile delinquency convictions was about 30 per cent greater in the first year of the war than in the preceding year, with an increase of 41 per cent for children under fourteen and 22 per cent for children fourteen to sixteen. As evidence of the effects of the present war on juveniles this reported increase should be discounted somewhat because juvenile delinquency convictions had a decided upward trend during the preceding decade. From 1929 to 1938 the number of male juvenile convictions for indictable crimes per 100,000 in each age group in England increased 129 per cent for children under fourteen, 82 per cent for those fourteen to sixteen, and 57 per cent for those sixteen to twenty-one. Approximately one-third of the increase in the first year of the war would have been expected if the trend of the preceding decade had continued and no war had occurred. This leaves a substantial increase in juvenile convictions above the trend.

World War I provides more complete information on the trend in juvenile convictions. Compared with the pre-war years 1910–13 juvenile convictions in 1914–18 increased 69 per cent in England, 63 per cent in Germany, and 52 per cent in Austria. The increase began immediately after the outbreak of the war and rose steadily until the end of the war. This reinforces the scattered evidence regarding the trend in the present war and supports a prediction that juvenile convictions will increase during the remainder of this war.

The trend in the convictions of women in the first World War was similar to that of juveniles. Female convictions in 1914–18 were 52 per cent higher than in 1910–13 in Germany, 80 per cent higher in France, and 156 per cent higher in Austria. Their convictions decreased slightly during the first year of the war and thereafter rose steadily. One special study in Germany resulted in the conclusion that convictions of both men and women over fifty years of age increased, while another special study resulted in the conclusion that females under thirty had an increase in the number of convictions while those over thirty had a decrease.

From this evidence that the convictions of boys, girls, women, and perhaps of men over fifty increased, it may be inferred that the rate of conviction of men in the age group eighteen to fifty who remained in the civilian population and whose population base cannot be determined accurately also increased.

4. *Convictions by general classes of crimes.*—The decrease in the absolute number of convictions for all crimes is a resultant of two conflicting trends, namely, a decrease in the convictions for sex offenses and for attacks on the person (including murder, manslaughter, assaults, and, in Germany, slander and libel) and an increase in the convictions for thefts. The absolute number of convictions for sex offenses decreased 41 per cent in Germany, 48 per cent in England, and 68 per cent in Austria, and for attacks on the person decreased 23 per cent in Germany, 35 per cent in England, and 83 per cent in Austria. The absolute number of convictions for thefts increased 23 per cent in Austria and remained approximately constant in England and Germany, although several million young men were mobilized. Because of the uncertainty regarding the population base for men, the trends in these three types of crimes can be determined more satisfactorily by confining the analysis to the data regarding juveniles and women.

In Germany convictions of juveniles for thefts were 67 per cent higher in the war years than in the pre-war years, while convictions were 24 per cent lower for attacks on the person and 36 per cent lower for sex offenses. In Austria convictions of juveniles for thefts were 104 per cent higher in the war period while convictions for attacks on the person were 82 per cent lower and for sex offenses 68 per cent lower. In Germany the convictions of girls did not increase as much as the convictions of boys, but in Austria the convictions of girls increased 155 per cent and for boys only 37 per cent. In both Germany and Austria the convictions of girls for sex offenses decreased and the convictions for thefts increased. In the present war it has been reported from a few American cities and from England that the convictions of girls have increased more than the convictions of boys and that the increase in the convictions of girls is principally for sex offenses.

The convictions of women in Germany during the first World War went up 61 per cent for thefts and down 6 per cent for sex offenses and 17 per cent for attacks on the person.

5. *Convictions for minor crimes.*—The convictions for offenses usually regarded as minor changed from the pre-war level, either upward or downward, more than the convictions for offenses regarded as serious. In England the convictions for indictable crimes decreased only 10 per cent, while convictions for nonindictable crimes decreased 35 per cent. In Germany convictions for the most serious crimes (*Verbrechen*) decreased 18 per cent, for the intermediate crimes (*Vergehen*) 39 per cent, and for the least serious (*Übertretungen*) 63 per cent. The same difference appeared in Austria in less extreme form.

The difference between the trends in minor and major crimes appears, also, in some of the specific types of crimes. In England, Germany, and Austria the convictions for robbery, burglary, fraud, and embezzlement varied from the pre-war level by small amounts but for ordinary larcenies increased greatly. In England convictions for indictable sex offenses, principally incest, statutory or other rape, bigamy, and sex perversions, decreased only 5 per cent, while convictions for nonindictable sex offenses, principally prostitution, decreased 45 per cent. In Germany convictions of women for murder and manslaughter increased 4 per cent, while convictions for slander and libel decreased 33 per cent and for assaults decreased 19 per cent. Furthermore, assaults in Germany are divided into two classes:

convictions of women for minor assaults decreased 50 per cent while convictions of women for dangerous assaults decreased only 8 per cent.

6. *Post-war convictions.*—In the post-war period from 1919 to 1923 the number of convictions rose far above the pre-war level in Germany and Austria, while in England the number of convictions did not rise to the pre-war level until 1926. The number of convictions of women in the post-war period was 383 per cent above the pre-war level in Austria, 108 per cent in France, and 40 per cent in Germany. These increases in post-war convictions were for thefts; the convictions for most other offenses either remained on the low level of the war or dropped even lower. Post-war crime waves were reported also in France after the Revolution of 1848, in the United States after the Civil War, in Germany and Austria after the war of 1866, and in Germany and France after the Franco-Prussian War of 1870–71.

7. *Recidivism.*—Recidivism was recorded as decreasing in Germany and Austria during the first World War. In Germany 46 per cent of the persons convicted in 1910–13 were recorded as having been punished previously; this percentage decreased to 33 in 1914–18 and to 17 in 1919–23.

The seven preceding generalizations have been derived from the statistics of the criminal courts. I wish to add two generalizations derived from other sources.

8. *Special war laws.*—The number of infractions of special war laws in all the countries involved in the first World War and in the present war was enormous. These infractions usually receive official attention, if at all, from administrative boards and officers and seldom result in trials in the criminal courts. The number of cases under the special war laws which came before administrative boards in Vienna during the first World War exceeded the number of prosecutions in the criminal courts in the pre-war years. The black markets in Austria

were probably organized as thoroughly and patronized even more generally than the bootleg business in American cities during our prohibition period. Austrian banks often participated in the financing of this traffic in prohibited commodities. In the present war the violations of the special war laws are widespread in the countries at war. Newspapers recently reported an estimate by one of the administrative officers that four hundred thousand stores in the United States are violating the price-ceiling regulations. These violations of laws are crimes even if they are handled by administrative boards. If they are added to the convictions in criminal courts, they probably more than wipe out the decrease in the total conviction rate which was reported previously.

9. *White-collar crimes.*—The number of white-collar crimes in the United States during the first World War and during the first year of the present war was large—perhaps larger than in the preceding years. The principal white-collar crime in the first World War was known as "profiteering." This frequently took the form of fraudulent execution of cost-plus contracts, with extravagant padding of costs as a method of increasing profits. This was a corporate form of stealing. After the war several congressional committees investigated the profiteering which had occurred in the war and issued reports which contained not only indictments of the war profiteers but abundant evidence of the basis for the indictments. Some profiteers were prosecuted, but almost without exception they escaped conviction during a post-war administration which, as frequently happens in post-war periods, was unusually corrupt. Many contractors, however, were compelled by fear of prosecution to reimburse the government. The cost-plus contracts of the first World War produced such a bad odor when the facts became known that a decision was reached to refrain completely from cost-plus contracts in the event of a future war.

In the present war white-collar crimes have been brought to

public attention by several congressional committees and by federal boards and officers. These reports have made it clear that costs are again being padded enormously. Some corporations have been indicted for price-fixing and collusive bidding in violation of antitrust laws, and some corporations have been attempting to secure a moratorium on the criminal laws which apply specifically to themselves. Some manufacturing corporations have been convicted of bribing federal inspectors; one conviction of this nature was for bribing a federal inspector to accept defective explosives for the Army and Navy and another to accept defective parts for airplane engines. White-collar crimes have been reported in the United States in the present war in regard to ships, airplanes, explosives, ordnance, machine tools, army camps, army hats, many metals, and many kinds of food.

No centralized statistical index and few specialized indices of white-collar crimes are available. Consequently, it is not possible to make a precise comparison of the frequency of white-collar crimes in a war period and a pre-war period.

CONVICTION RATES AND CRIMINAL BEHAVIOR

The second part of this analysis is an appraisal of the preceding statistical generalizations in terms of the behavior of people. The changes in the number of convictions unquestionably reflect changes in the behavior of people. The question is: What behaviors do they reflect? They may reflect one or more of three behaviors.

First, they may reflect a change in the number of crimes committed. This is the interpretation which is usually made. According to this interpretation, an increase in convictions means that crimes increased and a decrease in convictions means that crimes decreased and that the ratio between convictions and crimes committed remains approximately constant. The two other interpretations which may be made are seldom considered.

Second, the changes in the statistical index may reflect the behavior of the clerks who keep the records. It is possible that the reported decrease in recidivism was due, not to a decrease in recidivism, but to the pressure of work upon the administrative personnel and the decrease in their competence in the war period, as a result of which they did not check the previous criminal records of persons who appeared before the courts as carefully as had been done in pre-war years. The significance of this interpretation is limited and for that reason will be disregarded in the subsequent discussion.

Third, changes in convictions may reflect changes in the reactions toward consummated criminal behavior by the public and by the administrative and judicial personnel. The decrease in the convictions for sex offenses may have been due to increased tolerance of illicit sex behavior, and the illicit sex behavior may in fact have been increasing while convictions were decreasing. Convictions for thefts may have increased in the war period because in that time of scarcity of commodities property owners resented the theft of property which they would have overlooked in pre-war years. Convictions of juvenile delinquents may have increased because parents and others did not have the time and energy to deal with problem behavior in wartime and on that account more quickly referred problem children to the public authorities. That tolerance, and the manner in which it is implemented, is a factor of great importance in the number of convictions may be inferred from the relatively great increases and decreases in convictions for minor offenses while convictions for major offenses remained relatively constant. The positions of various acts on the scale of values may change greatly in wartime. Relatively small thefts may be regarded by property owners as serious, and relatively small assaults may be regarded by the victims or the public as not worth bothering about. It is easy to understand the great changes in convictions for minor offenses in terms of the reactions of the public but not easy to understand them in terms of the behavior of offenders. It might be argued that, since men commit a larger proportion of serious offenses than of minor offenses, the convictions for minor offenses would swing further away from pre-war level than the convictions for serious offenses do because in wartime men are a smaller percentage of the persons convicted. This argument is untenable, however, when it is learned that convictions for minor offenses by women, considered separately, swing away from the pre-war level as much as do the convictions of the entire population and that convictions of women for serious offenses remain relatively constant.

A conviction rate is a function of two variables, namely, criminal behavior and reactions of others toward the consummated criminal behavior. An increase in convictions should not be assumed to reflect an increase in crimes or a decrease in tolerance; the relationship must be determined by investigation. The separation of these two variables in the conviction rate is not easy, perhaps not possible. Until they are separated, the conviction rates are not a good index of criminal behavior.

A rough appraisal of the importance of each of the variables can be made if we have sufficient descriptive information regarding the countries at war. We know that alcohol was very scarce, that the number of admissions of patients with alcoholic psychoses to hospitals for the insane decreased, and that deaths due to diseases usually ascribed to alcohol decreased. With this supplementary information we can feel fairly certain that the decrease in the number of convictions for drunkenness reflected an actual decrease in drunkenness, although it is still possible that the proportion of cases of drunkenness which resulted in convictions was not the same as in the pre-war period.

Although convictions for sex offenses decreased in the countries at war, the descriptive accounts include many references to increases in illicit sex behavior, and some statistical data support these descriptions. In Germany the percentage of all births that were illegitimate increased from 9.4 a year in 1910–13 to 13.1 in 1918. The number of convictions for abortion increased in England, Germany, and Austria; the number of convictions for concealing childbirth increased in England; and the number of convictions for child murder increased in Germany. This supplementary information leads one to suspect that even though convictions for sex offenses were decreasing, illicit sex behavior was increasing.

The descriptive accounts of social life in Germany and Austria during the first World War include many references to thefts. The thefts were directed at commodities more than in pre-war years and less at money. Some thefts were mass raids on farms and gardens. In Austria on one occasion two hundred persons went to the country with carts, bags, and other containers and were collecting food where they could find it when the police appeared and succeeded in arresting twenty-four of them. Gangs were reported to be more numerous and larger and, to some extent, to have better organized techniques. Gangs of boys and girls at first stole coal from cars standing on the railway tracks, later by breaking signal lights so that the trains were compelled to run slowly and they could climb on the trains and throw off the coal. These descriptive accounts give support to the reported increases in convictions for theft.

These descriptive accounts, however, are not always a safe basis for interpreting the statistics of convictions. We know that gasoline and automobiles were scarce in all the countries in the first World War. For that reason we expect a decrease in the convictions under the highway acts. A person who consults the English criminal statistics with this expectation is surprised to learn that convictions under the highway acts, instead of decreasing, increased about 15 per cent in the war period. He must then search for an explanation of the increase instead of the expected decrease. Fortunately the English statistics give details of convictions under the highway acts which facilitate an interpretation. The 15 per cent increase was made up as follows: convictions decreased 35 per cent for obstructions and nuisances in the highways and 20 per cent for offenses connected with locomotives, and increased 8 per cent for offenses connected with carts, 32 per cent for motorcars, and 80 per cent for bicycles. Although this does not explain the increase in convictions connected with motorcars, it does suggest that the increased use of bicycles during the war explains the increase in the total convictions. If convictions connected with bicycles are eliminated both in the war period and in the pre-war period, the remaining convictions under the highway acts were more numerous in the pre-war period than in the war period.

THEORIES OF WARTIME CRIME

I shall consider in this final section some of the theories of criminal behavior in wartime. Any explanatory generalization regarding crime in wartime is suspect because neither war nor crime is a homogeneous entity. Wars vary widely in many respects, and the constituent elements have not been standardized, nor have their comparative weights in the total complex of war been determined. Consequently, we do not know, even approximately, how much more war is involved in one war than in another. Also, many social changes which occur in wars occur also in times of peace. For these reasons the effect of wars on crimes is not a good theoretical problem.

Criticism of general theories.—All the special theories of criminal behavior in wartime should be regarded as invalid, inadequate, or unproved for one or more reasons. First, when one theory makes assumptions in direct conflict with the assumptions of another theory, one must be wrong. One theory states that war produces an increase in crimes because of the emotional instability in wartime and another states that wars produce a decrease in crimes because of an upsurge of national feeling. One theory states that crimes of violence increase in wartime because of the contagion of violence, and another that they decrease because of the vicarious satiation of the need for violence. Their assumptions of fact are in conflict, and one of the theories must be wrong unless the statements are limited to defined areas of behavior, and this limitation is not stated.

Second, the theories which assume explicitly or implicitly that the several types of crimes increase or decrease uniformly are in conflict with the statistics of convictions and, at least, are not proved. One theory explains an assumed increase in crimes by emotional instability but makes no effort to explain why emotionally unstable people have more convictions for one type of crime and fewer convictions for another type of crime than emotionally stable people did before the war. Similarly, the theories of the diminishing role of the future or the upsurge of national feelings do not explain why convictions for some crimes increase and for others decrease.

Third, a theory of criminal behavior which is directed at individual variations is of little value in explaining the abrupt and enormous changes in conviction rates. The psychogenic theories, which explain deviate behavior in adult life by early childhood experiences, are not adapted to the explanation of these mass movements, but they should be consistent with the theories which do explain them.

Fourth, all the special theories of criminal behavior in wartime can be questioned because they fail to allow for variations in tolerance toward consummated criminal behavior. The more careful students make general criticisms of the criminal statistics, but they then proceed to use convictions as approximate indicators of criminal behavior. An adequate theory of criminal behavior must separate these two variables in the data. Also, an adequate theory should explain changes in criminal behavior and changes in the reactions toward criminal behavior in the same general terms, although not usually as applying to the same individuals. Both criminal behavior and reactions to criminal behavior are expressions of attitudes toward criminal codes and toward the concrete values which the codes are designed to protect, and generalizations which apply to one should apply also to the other.

The preceding criticisms of the theories of criminal behavior in wartime do not mean that the factors of contagion of violence, satiation of the need for violence, the diminishing role of the future, and national feeling have no effect on behavior. The criticisms mean rather that the respects in which these factors play a part have not been defined, the relations of these factors to one another have not been determined, and the factors have not been organized into a system of thought.

Exner's theory.—If the changes in criminal behavior were separated from the changes in the reactions to criminal behavior, we would still have the problem of determining what factors and what organization of factors explain the changes in criminal behavior. In the discussion of this question I shall accept for the moment the usual assumption that convictions are an approximately accurate index of criminal behavior and consider one of the more adequate theories, which makes the same assumption. This is the theory of Exner, based on his study of crime in Austria during the first World War. His theory is that the scarcity of commodities explains both the increase in thefts and the decrease in sex offenses and assaults; thefts increased because of the pressure of unsatisfied needs and the restrictions on legitimate methods of securing commodities; sex offenses and assaults decreased because the undernourished people had little surplus energy for sex offenses and assaults; included in the scarce commodities was alcohol, and the decrease in sex offenses and assaults was affected especially by the scarcity of this commodity.

This theory has the advantage of providing a unified explanation of the increases in some crimes and decreases in other crimes. Obviously it fits many of the facts, for in many ways convictions for thefts changed concomitantly with changes in economic distress. As a first approximation to an explanatory generalization it is much better than the other theories. The crucial question, as far as thefts are concerned, is: Does this theory mean that thefts would not increase in a country at war if economic distress did not increase, even though all the other changes of wartime did occur? This meaning is implied in the theory, although Exner does not state it explicitly.

When the theory is inspected from this point of view, it does not fit some of the facts. First, convictions for thefts increased in England by approximately the same percentage as in Germany and Austria, although economic distress was much less in England than in Germany and Austria. Second, thefts increased in Canada during the war, although economic distress decreased. Third, thefts by children began to increase in each of the countries immediately after the outbreak of the war, although there was little economic distress in the first months of the war. Fourth, thefts by children increased more than thefts by adults in England, Germany, and Austria, although children were probably in no greater distress than adults. Fifth, juvenile thefts are probably increasing in the United States during the present war, although economic distress is decreasing. Sixth, over long periods of time variations in convictions for thefts and variations in the business cycle have a very low coefficient of correlation. Seventh, members of the white-collar class commit many thefts in the form of fraud, although they do not suffer economic distress in the sense in which that term is used with reference to Germany and Austria in the war period.

Differential organization as an explanation.—A clue to a more adequate explanation of thefts in wartime is provided by the ecological studies of crime in American cities. These studies show that crime is closely associated with poverty by residential areas, in contrast with the studies of time series, which show that crime has very little association with poverty by chronological periods. Poverty, as such, cannot be important in the causation of crime when poverty is arranged by geographic units and unimportant when poverty is arranged by chronological units. Something must be associated with poverty when it is considered geographically and not associated with poverty when it is considered chronologically. If this something can be abstracted from poverty and related directly to crime, we may be able to find a more consistent relationship. This something is probably the contacts and communications of people, for these do not change appreciably in the business cycle but do change greatly with mobility from one residential area to another. These contacts and communications may vary independently of poverty. For this reason we find very low juvenile delinquency rates in certain segregated groups, especially the oriental groups in American cities, which live in poverty in areas which have high delinquency rates.

We may then ask: What other things were connected with the economic distress which Exner regarded as the cause of the increase in thefts? The following are some of these. First, the external opportunities for thefts increased because the owners of property spent a larger part of their time away from home, because supervision in industrial and commercial establishments decreased, because the railways carried increased loads of commodities without increase in the number of guards, because a large number of persons, not selected on the basis of trustworthiness, were placed in positions of responsibility, and because the police force decreased in number and training. Second, the efforts to train children and adults in opposition to stealing were relaxed or abandoned because parents were away from home and because schools and churches were closed or were diverted to other purposes. Third, many persons, especially younger children, were left in complete idleness with no provision for supervised legal activities. Fourth, many of the poor people developed increased hostility toward some property owners who were regarded as hoarders or owners of goods by other illegal methods. Fifth, the meaning of property ownership and of property rights was confused by governmental appropriation of private property, by radical departures from the previous system of determining values and distributing property, and by general use of public property with little attention to its ownership. Sixth, contacts with criminal patterns were increased because of the passage of large numbers of children and women from the sheltered environment of the home to the heterogeneous environment of the factory, shop, and store, because of the great increase in the mobility of people, and because persons who had been stealing previously now stole with increased frequency and thus more effectively presented the patterns of theft to the nonthieves. Seventh, many public and private employees, especially railway employees, were in collusion with the thieves. Eighth, many persons who were not in economic distress were engaged systematically in stealing for the black markets. Ninth, a situation had occurred which was appropriate for theft according to the cultural definition which had been held for a long time and somewhat generally, namely, the situation in which theft is the only apparent alternative to starvation.

The first five of these changes are aspects of the breakdown of the organization for the prevention of thefts and refer primarily to those who react against prospective and consummated thefts; the last four are aspects of the organization for thefts and refer primarily to those who steal. The two groups of factors together may be called differential group organization. Many of these items may change in a country at war which has no economic distress and may result in nearly as much increase in thefts as in the country which is in economic distress.

Limitations of time prevent a similar analysis of the decrease in convictions for sex offenses and assaults, and of the factor of tolerance, which was waived for purposes of the present analysis and which is one aspect of the reaction to consummated crimes. Even if time permitted, a continuation of the analysis would do little more than provide additional illustrations of the possibility of organizing the multiple factors into a somewhat unified system of thought.

This system of thought may be formulated with reference to any type of crime as follows: A conviction rate is a function of two variables, namely, criminal behavior and reactions against criminal behavior; each of these is an expression of changes in group organization, as is also the conviction rate; the two aspects of organization together are called differential group organization. The balance between the opposed organizations determines whether the crimes committed, the reactions against crimes, and the conviction rates increase or decrease.

In order to clarify the meaning of this proposition, a few explanations are needed. First, organization has two principal constituent elements, namely, consensus in regard to objectives and implementation for the realization of objectives. Each of these may vary independently of the other, but they usually vary together. Each of these is found in the organization for crime and the organization against crime.

Second, the phrase "differential group organization" is used here with reference to a specific behavior. Although a nation may become thoroughly disorganized and all kinds of behavior may reflect this general disorganization, the usual change is the breakdown of organization for one kind of behavior while organization for another kind of behavior is developing. Organization for war purposes is developing in our country at present while organization for certain familial behaviors is breaking down. Similarly, organization for stealing may be developing and organization against stealing breaking down, while organization for drunkenness is breaking down and organization against drunkenness is developing.

Third, the abstract principle of differential group organization should be universally associated with these changes in conviction rates in wartime although any specific condition involved in the differential group organization may occur with greater or less frequency. The relationship between the abstract principle and the concrete conditions may be illustrated by the variations in the family conditions of delinquents. Some delinquents have cruel stepmothers and others have conscientious and religious mothers who are almost completely ignorant of the conditions of life in American cities. The abstract principle in both is that the mother is not effective in training and supervising her children; the concrete ways in which that principle appears may vary widely. This relationship between abstract principle and concrete conditions is found throughout the whole range of conditions which are related to criminal behavior in wartime.

Fourth, a statement of crime in wartime in terms of differential organization does not explain why the organizations change. The proposition is a hypothetical statement of a uniformity, but it does not attempt to explain the entire chain of events preceding the criminal behavior.

I have referred to this proposed method of explaining

changes in criminal behavior in wartime as a hypothesis. It is, obviously, not a precise proposition that can be easily tested and pronounced right or wrong; probably "hypothesis" is not the correct name for the proposition. It is an orientation rather than a definite hypothesis. Probably a precise hypothesis regarding the effect of wars upon criminal behavior cannot be stated, because this is not a precise theoretical problem.

If this orientation toward the problem of the effect of war on criminal behavior is justified, it eliminates certain other approaches. One of the theories which would be eliminated is the psychogenic theory that criminal behavior is rooted in early childhood experiences and appears in later life by a process of maturation. That theory, obviously, is not an explanation of the sudden mass movements revealed by criminal statistics. It seems necessary, however, that any theory which is valid in the explanation of individual differences in criminal behavior be consistent with a theory which is valid for these mass movements in criminal behavior. Another orientation toward the effects of wars on criminal behavior which is eliminated if differential group organization is a justifiable orientation is a theory which makes an explanation in terms of a particular concrete condition, such as poverty. The theory which is suggested uses poverty as a part of the explanation but does so by abstracting from poverty and other concrete conditions a general principle that should be universally associated with the changes in crime rates.

BIBLIOGRAPHY

EXNER, FRANZ. *Krieg und Kriminalität in Österreich*. Carnegie Institute for International Peace, "Economic and Social History of the World War," ed. JAMES T. SHOTWELL. Vienna, 1927.

GLUECK, ELEANOR T. "Wartime Delinquency," *Journal of Criminal Law and Criminology*, XXXIII (July, 1942), 119–35.

LIEPMANN, MORITZ. *Krieg und Kriminalität in Deutschland*. Carnegie

Institute for International Peace, "Economic and Social History of the World War," ed. James T. Shotwell. Stuttgart, 1930.

Mannheim, Hermann. *War and Crime*. London, 1941.

———. *Social Aspects of Crime in England between the Wars*. London, 1940.

Reckless, Walter C. "The Impact of War on Crime, Delinquency, and Prostitution," *American Journal of Sociology*, XLVIII (November, 1942), 378–86.

Rosenblum, Betty B. "The Relationship between War and Crime in the United States," *Journal of Criminal Law and Criminology*, XXX (January, 1940), 722–40.

Starke, W. *Verbrechen und Verbrecher in Preussen, 1854–78*. Berlin, 1884.

MORALE

HERBERT BLUMER

☼

THE STATE OF THE PROBLEM

MODERN war has made morale a consideration of primary importance. The formation of huge conscript armies in place of professional, mercenary, or volunteer forces has compelled attention to the so-called spiritual factor. There is need of developing among conscript soldiery a spirit to fill the place of what is otherwise accomplished by habit, interest, and wish. The appearance of so-called total warfare has led to a similar concern. The enlistment of all citizens in the war effort and the subordination of their institutions to this enterprise set a problem of developing allegiance, of implanting convictions, and of establishing a new outlook. The development of "psychological warfare" has further spotlighted the problem of morale. The use of propaganda, doctored news, falsified information, rumor, and deceptive publicity to arouse dissension and to undermine faith has now become a familiar story. Before such aggressive and insinuating attacks warring nations find it necessary to bulwark the allegiance and determination of their citizenry.

It is such characteristic features of modern war which have set the problem of morale and made it a matter of conspicuous concern. While military leaders throughout history have been somewhat cognizant of a problem of morale, the problem, until recent times, has been casual and not of much conscious interest. This has been due likely to the fact that in most collective undertakings the formation of morale is spontaneous, and the requisite devices for its guidance are contained in the natural ways of living of the group. The primitive tribe, the religious sect, the band of fighters, the small professional army—all develop naturally the spirit of unity and the fortification of effort essential to their tasks. There is little occasion for morale to become a pressing problem. In our modern life the setting is markedly different; it is that of a large aggregate society whose members have distant and remote relations and possess different values and problems. In such a society people do not have the same purpose and the intimate sense of mutual support that make morale a spontaneous matter in a common group or natural community.

The introduction of a huge enterprise such as a war effort in a modern society is confronted with such a setting. It is a problem of forming collective conduct among individuated people in new, unusual, and artificial relations without the benefit of the inspiration and control of a congenial group. This task involves the development of favorable attitudes and sentiments, of outlooks and points of view, of a spirit of mutual purpose, and of co-operation.

The interest in the topic of morale, as we all know, has become widespread. The term has become popular and loaded with honorific meaning. Accordingly, it has been appropriated by different people for amazingly diverse purposes and used to justify countless proposals which their authors regarded as beneficial. This has operated to make the term vague and confused—a vagueness and confusion which have carried over into the academic and scientific fields. Workers in the psychological and social sciences have been particularly eager to employ the term. Seemingly, they have been content to start with a specious and obvious notion of it and then to develop conceptions suitable to their interests and biases. The result has been to make its meaning and understanding con-

fused and to lead to a variety of amazing proposals as to how
morale should be established. The situation has been sufficiently bad to make a number of students altogether sus-
picious of the "scientific" value of the idea of morale and resolved to have nothing to do with it.

The picture, on one hand, of the importance of the conditions which have set the problem of morale and, on the other,
of the confused notions of morale makes it necessary to try to
clarify the term. This I propose to do in a rather lengthy consideration of the nature of morale.

THE NATURE OF MORALE

My purpose is to discuss the rudimentary yet fundamental
features of group morale—morale as an organization of collective intention rather than as a form of experience in the individual. One can get a clear understanding of its character by
analyzing the simple circumstance or condition in which it
arises. This circumstance is that in which a group is striving
to realize a collective goal. The goal may be that of surviving
in the face of catastrophe like a defeat in battle, a pestilence,
or a severe impairment of food supply; it may be that of attain-
ing conquest over some territory or peoples; it may be that of a
realization of a reform or revolutionary program; it may be
that of being successful in some expedition. Indeed, the circumstance occasioning morale exists whenever any group of
human beings undertakes to engage in some enterprise. Nations
at war, armies, religious sects, reform movements, revolutionary movements, political parties, exploring expeditions, a
band of mountain climbers, a corps of scientific workers, foot-
ball teams, a hunting expedition, a group of children making a
boat—these are just a few of countless group enterprises in
which morale has its natural setting.

In reflecting on the generic situation of group morale, namely, a collective enterprise, one can see clearly two fundamental

features: the relation of the group toward its goal and the relation of the members of the group to one another. The ability of a group to realize an objective or goal depends on the intensity of its inclination toward that goal and on its capacity of sticking together as a group. Morale centers around these two features. Where morale is high, there is a persistence in carrying out the task of the group and a willingness to stick together on behalf of the group cause. Morale is poor when there is little attachment to the goal and where there is no effective willingness toward joint undertaking. Morale is undermined when adherence to the goal is lessened, as through disheartenment, and where there is a break in the spirit of cooperation, as through dissension. These two features of intention and co-operation may be readily translated into the moral traits which bulk so large in the current thinking on morale. Corresponding to the effort on behalf of the goal are such traits as determination, courage, stubbornness, fortitude, will to persist, stoutheartedness, and the refusal to quit. Corresponding to the mutual relations of the members are qualities of allegiance, loyalty, spirit of co-operation, camaraderie, and fellowship.

It should be noted that these two fundamental factors—group intention and co-operation—do not exist as items separate from each other. They are intimately related, with each dependent on the other and each fortifying the other. If the members of a group develop a collective goal which is highly valued, they become much more disposed to camaraderie and fellowship. Conversely, if the members have a strong feeling of common identification, and sense in one another congeniality and a readiness to mutual aid, there are imparted extra significance and value to the goal. This reciprocal relation between common goal and fellow-feeling brings out the important point that group morale is a collective product and that it is shared. It is a collective product in the sense that it arises from the response of persons to one another and to symbols of one another; the image which the members have of the group goal is dependent on the way in which the goal is pictured to them by the actions and expressions of one another. It is shared in that it is formed out of mutual stimulation and re-inforcement. *Group morale exists as a disposition to act together toward a goal.*

This statement of group morale in terms of its two funda-mental features of purpose and co-operation is simple and is essentially a truism. Yet it provides us with the fundamental ideas necessary for the understanding of morale and for the analysis of particular forms of morale. In the light of it, it is possible to note a number of things on which there is much confused thinking.

First, it should be realized that morale can be organized around very different collective goals—around aims that em-body very different conceptions of life and widely diverse sets of ideals. Morale can be very high in groups whose objectives impress us as bizarre, superstitious, idiotic, or immoral. A re-ligious sect, such as the Millerites, in the face of ridicule, contempt, and persecution may persist in the preparation for the millennial day when they may ascend to heaven in white robes. The Fuzzy-Wuzzies with their primitive spears and bows and arrows may hurl themselves in suicidal effort into devastating rifle fire. A band of pirates may plunge into a cam-paign of murder, destruction, and pillage with the highest of morale. The peoples of a dictatorship may sacrifice life, prop-erty, and individual independence most readily and retain a staunch purpose. It is erroneous to believe that morale pre-supposes that people possess a noble doctrine, a highly moral philosophy, or a code of Christian ethics. Similarly, it is faulty to believe that good morale requires a certain kind of moral person. Morale, in a collective undertaking, may be high among all types and levels of people—the good, the bad, the arrogant, the humble, the depraved, the cultured, the illiterate, the intelligent, the stupid, the learned, and the ignorant. For all that is basically necessary for morale is that the people in a group have a goal which they value highly and seek eagerly and a sense of mutual support in their effort to attain it.

Next it may be noted that morale exists with reference to a particular collective enterprise—with reference to the particular group task. There is, it is true, some sense in speaking of what Hocking aptly terms a "morale of being"[1]—a general state of readiness of a people to begin with spirit a wide range of undertakings. This is akin to the physical tone of the body in a healthy athlete; in the group it is present in the form of a tradition to accomplish things and of a customary practice of energetic action. Despite the significance of such a general readiness to morale, it is nevertheless true that the morale of people is contingent on the particular way in which they view the goal of an undertaking. The same group may have high morale for one kind of enterprise and a very weak morale for a different kind of undertaking. In war effort the group may act with strong morale; in the reorganization of a peacetime society it may have markedly poor morale. This is no more than saying that people will act together with vigor and determination when "their heart" is in the enterprise. This point is painfully simple but needs to be appreciated.

In the light of it we must realize that *any* people, irrespective of race, nationality, economic condition, or state of culture, may have high morale if the collective enterprise to which they are committed enlists completely their hopes, fervent wishes, and aspirations. The primitives in the African jungles, the peons in a plantation economy, the slaves in a rigid caste order, the proletariat of the slums, any nationality—Italian,

---

[1] William Hocking, "The Nature of Morale," *American Journal of Sociology*, XLVII, No. 3 (November, 1941), 302–20.

Poles, Danes, Frenchmen—any race, or any religious people may develop high morale in some particular undertaking. The same group of people may show amazing morale in one situation; in another it may be devoid of morale.

Another commonplace point that follows from the discussion so far is that morale is a product of experience. It is indeed rare for a group to form almost spontaneously a collective goal charged with high value and to develop instantaneously a sense of mutual support among its members. Some crises, such as an immoral attack, may quickly arouse such a disposition. Usually, however, the group has to build up its goal, forming an image of its position and of its task out of continuing experience. It is a process of growth and learning, of changed views and assessments of the group aim, of transformation of the conceptions which the people have of themselves with reference to the collective undertaking. People usually have to form and re-form their images of the goal, discover and rediscover their group, develop and redevelop their allegiance. The line of experience may be long and it may be bitter. High morale, in the form of a fixity of purpose and an abiding sense of unity, is forged out of a complicated process of definition and redefinition of goal, of evaluation and revaluation of event, until there is a common understanding imbedded in the feelings and images of the people. Morale is not something already made, merely to be pumped into people. It is not, as Hocking points out, something that is manufactured in the psychological workshop. It is not induced by the mere application of so-called psychological laws apart from experience in the collective enterprise. The most conspicuous cases of morale in history have occurred without the benefit of psychologists.

The historical background of the people, the kind of events in their experience, the way in which these events are interpreted, the singularity of their goal, of their interests, intentions, and self-conceptions—all point to the uniqueness of the structure of morale in different situations. We may note this in the significant difference between the morale structures in present-day China, Japan, Soviet Russia, Germany, and England. Such a commonplace point needs to be mentioned in the face of current notions that morale is something to be produced by a series of techniques, tricks, and formulas.

Finally, passing reference should be made to the often mentioned point that the test of morale is the ability of the group to meet adverse circumstance. The strength of morale is indicated by the disposition to persist in the face of setbacks, arduous circumstances, reverses, and defeats. A collective enterprise moving along without difficulty or opposition requires no high order of morale. And, incidentally, sampling of a group in such a condition may easily yield a fallacious picture of the state and degree of morale. An estimation of the morale of a group in advance of the test of adversity should be in terms of factors that refer to persistent effort, something, incidentally, not easily accomplished by so-called morale tests now popular among psychologists. We might bear in mind the comment of Wellington on the Battle of Waterloo: "The French and English soldiers were equally brave at Waterloo; the English were brave five minutes longer."

INADEQUATE VIEWS OF MORALE

Realizing that morale exists in the disposition of a group to act together toward a goal and that its vigor depends on how vitally the goal is framed, we can consider a number of current views of morale and recommendations for its formation which seem inadequate.

First of all, we should note that it is distinctly conceivable, although unlikely, that a collective enterprise, with even the huge dimensions of winning a national war, may be carried on effectively with a minimum of morale. A group, such as a nation, may have an equipment fully adequate for the task, an efficient organization, and a trained and skilful personnel. The participation of the people in such an enterprise may occur as a matter of course. It may be brought about by force or coercion, by mere habituation to assigned tasks, or by matter-of-fact obedience. In such an efficiently organized effort there may be little need for the group to be strongly animated by a common goal or to feel keenly any participation in mutual effort. The features of technological organization and efficient skills, of equipment and strength, *may* lessen dependency on morale.

Conversely, one should realize that a group with a high morale may fail in a collective task because of the absence of equipment, techniques and skills, or numbers. The disintegration of primitive tribes in the face of European aggression presents a pathetic panorama of such instances. Consequently, while the importance of morale in group undertakings is self-evident, one should view it in proper perspective and realize that it may not be effective under certain conditions and that under other conditions it may not be required.

One of the most widespread and least considerate conceptions of morale is the idea that morale results from a surcease from strain and labor. The view is that the spirit of people is kept high if they are provided with entertainment, amusement, and the facilities of relaxation. The arrangement for shows, theatrical performances, dance bands, reading material, athletic contests, dances, and socials ranks high, as we all know, in current efforts to establish morale. The ordinary morale officer in the armed services, I suspect, thinks primarily in terms of these things in carrying out his task. The view is prominent likewise in efforts to form civilian morale. Without minimizing the value of relaxation and fun for mental balance, or the way in which the efforts to provide them may give an impression of the interest of other people in one's welfare, it is clear that they do not meet what is crucial in group morale. This crucial feature is the formation of a highly valued goal. Such efforts characteristically are not directed to such a purpose.

Another view very much in the forefront of thinking and effort today is that morale is to be achieved through the formation of individual character. The belief is that if individuals have courage, faith, determination, and self-confidence, a high morale will automatically emerge in the group. Hence there is resort to exhortation, sermonizing, and education to inculcate such moral virtues in individuals. Again, it seems that such efforts, however commendable ethically, miss what is essential in morale. Individuals may be brave, determined, and self-confident and yet have little interest in or desire for a given collective goal. Under such circumstances they would have slight morale. The formation of an inspired goal in the case of a group may lead to courage, faith, and determination on the part of individuals; there are no evidence and no reason to believe that such traits in individuals will lead to an inspired group goal.

Still another idea of morale widely current these days in both lay and professional circles is that it comes in *adjusting* people to their life-situations and circumstances. If effective and happy adjustment is secured, morale is established. With this view morale effort becomes a matter of removing grievances, softening hardships, and establishing happy social relations. The faith in adjustment as the means to morale is perhaps most conspicuous in persons dealing with maladjusted people—as in social workers—but it is also prominent in other groups. In the case of this view I wish to note, again, a failure to touch what is central in collective morale. It is easy to conceive of a group of well-adjusted individuals hopelessly weak in morale in a given collective undertaking. If the individuals have little heart in the undertaking, their condition of happy adjustment is of little value. Adjustment is not the gateway to collective morale. The converse is much more likely to be true. People animated strongly by a common aim have an impressive way of enduring hardship and bearing grievance. Individual discomfort recedes before strong collective purpose.

The same point applies to another prominent notion of morale, namely, the view that morale is formed through a program of mental hygiene. This view is pronounced among psychiatrists and has become popular through the efforts of some psychiatrists to give "expert" recommendations on the formation of morale. In brief, the view is that morale is achieved if people are prepared to cope with anxiety and to avoid panic. Those who propose this view seem to hold before their eyes a picture such as the bombing of London or the flight of the French before the German armies. What is essential, it is felt, is to maintain a clear head and a poise of feeling. However plausible and sensible this view may seem, it does not deal with what is central in morale. A group of sane and mentally well-balanced individuals has no guaranty of developing morale. Their preparation for anxiety and panic is not the means of developing a strongly determined goal. It is rather the existence of such a goal which is the most effective preventative of anxiety and panic.

If space permitted, there might be added discussion of other current views of morale such as that it is to be achieved through rigorous discipline, through the development of a spirit of toughness, through the development of good leadership, through the stimulation of hatred, and through the generation of emotional enthusiasm. All these views, it seems to me, suffer from the same general type of confusion—in taking resultant and concomitant features of morale as central and in believing that the formation of these features will create morale. Instead, I would turn to the simple and truistic statement made earlier—that morale is the disposition of a group to act together toward a collective goal and that accordingly its strength depends on how the goal is conceived, on the feelings and interests developed around it, and on the mutual support which the members sense in one another. If the goal is vital and the sense of mutual effort strong, morale is high. It is not necessary for the people to have a clear understanding of the value of their goal—all that is necessary is that they sense or feel its importance. It seems clear that the development of morale centers around the process of defining and forming the goal and around the cultivation of the sense of common effort. The judgment and assessment of morale should be made in terms of this picture.

FORMS OF MORALE

If we view morale from the standpoint of the way in which the group has come to frame the goal of its undertaking, it is possible to distinguish several significant forms. There are three forms that merit discussion.

The first is where the goal is of rational expediency and hence where its achievement is of practical necessity. The demands of a situation may be such as to compel a group of people to stick steadfastly to a common aim because of practical necessity. The bands of pioneers threading their way across the hazardous plains illustrate this form of morale. The defense by crew and passengers on a ship against an attack by pirates was a common instance of this type of morale. A village, community, people, or nation endangered by aggressive attack of outsiders develops usually this kind of morale. Their goal is forced on them by the necessities of their situation; their consecration of effort to it is caused by practical expediency. This kind of morale occurs chiefly in groups whose collective enterprise is one of defense. But it is to be found also in other kinds of situations, as in the case of professional groups whose code requires them to persist in certain tasks despite unfavorable and adverse conditions. Doctors, soldiers, firemen, nurses, bandits, policemen, sailors, and miners may carry out a hazardous collective undertaking solely because its performance is conceived by them as something that has to be done. These various instances suggest, then, that the goal is one of practical necessity. The fact that the goal has a practical or expedient character does not mean that the morale need be low or feeble. If the goal is regarded as of high necessity, the intention and determination of the group to attain it may be very firm, and the sense of mutual responsibility in this task may be great.

This form of morale has its own unique character, and its formation is through means quite different from those in the other two forms of morale which I will shortly discuss. Where it is necessary to form practical morale consciously, it has to be done by making clear to people their situation and interpreting their common position and duty in such a way that the task is viewed as one of practical necessity. The beating of tom-toms, the resort to stratagems, the reliance on emotional appeals, and the evocation of religious sanctions are essentially irrelevant. Instead, the method is one of intelligent interpretation.

This form of morale has the advantage of not suffering from illusion. However, certain disadvantageous features should be noted. It is lacking in the dynamic impulsion that comes when the goal has a transcendental character. Further, the morale is likely to decay when the practical necessity of the goal is no longer felt, or if the successful attainment of the goal seems increasingly certain.

A second form of morale which can be distinguished develops around a romantic goal. The goal is colored with a variety of emotional and imaginative qualities which make it appealing, magnetic, and glorious. These qualities may stand for such diverse things as gain, loot, booty, riches, prestige, power, adventure, achievement, a new position in society, or a new social order. The El Dorado in the case of bands of Spanish adventurers, the recapture of the Holy Land in the case of the Crusaders, the prospect of loot in the case of predatory nomads, the prospect of power and glory in the instance of a band of political adventurers, the picture of international prestige and influence in a nationalistic movement, and the vision of a millennial order in the case of revolutionary movements—such are instances of romantic goals.

It is clear that the morale developed in such collective enterprises is significantly different from that where the goal is of practical necessity. It occurs usually in expansionist and aggressive collective enterprises. Because the goal stands for new achievement, the spirit of people is enlivened. They form a new, elevated conception of themselves or reaffirm previous exalted self-conceptions. The goal acquires a transcendental nature and yields a dynamic impulsion. In the development of the romantic goal or in the formation of the kind of morale that corresponds to it there is a legitimate place for myth creation and illusory coloration. The goal must be overvalued in the sense of having a character which numbs people to practical consequences and to ordinary private judgments. In deliberate effort to form such a kind of morale, emphasis must be given to the depiction of the romantic certainties and opportunities of the future—not to the practical necessities of the present.

The third and perhaps the most vital form of morale arises when the goal is sacred. The goal represents the primary as well as the ultimate value in life; its achievement becomes a matter of irrevocable duty and of divine injunction. As one would suspect, this type of morale is to be found most noticeably in the case of religious sects and movements. From the early Christian bands down to the contemporary Jehovah's Witnesses there have been innumerable instances of sectarian groups showing the most dogged persistence in the face of ridicule, punishment, hardship, deprivation, assault, and loss of life. This attachment to a sacred objective may be found also in the case of certain reform movements—more frequently in the case of revolutionary parties. It may arise in other groups—even in a national or racial people. Apparently, it is the type of morale in present-day Japan.

The rudiments of morale where the goal is sacred are easily discernible. They exist in the form of a set of convictions and a set of myths. Since the goal is sacred, people have a conviction of its supreme rectitude which renders them impervious to critical reflection upon its character or value. Since the goal is sensed as supremely perfect and accordingly in harmony with the true nature of the universe, people are convinced that its attainment is inevitable. Obstacles, delays, reversals, defeats, and frustrations become merely the occasion for renewed effort just because ultimate success is bound to occur. Finally, there is the conviction of being intrusted with a sacred mission. Because of the supreme value of the goal, because of the divine sanction which it implies, the people attached to the goal feel a sacred responsibility for its realization. They have a cause. They feel themselves to be a select group, especially chosen to execute a transcendental mission. With such convictions and self-conceptions a group is likely to develop an amazing determination in its quest and a striking cohesion in its ranks.

It is clear that the development of the sacred goal and the formation of morale corresponding to it are different from that of the practical goal or the romantic goal. The method is fundamentally the reaffirmation of myths and the fortification of a fixed conception which the people have of their destiny.

These three types of morale—the practical, the romantic, and the sacred—seem to me to be the fundamental forms. In any given instance of collective enterprise all three types may be present, with different people in the group framing the goal in different ways. However, it is almost certain that one of the types will be dominant—dominant to the point of being almost exclusive.

It should be realized that each type requires a special soil in which to grow—a soil set by the traditional background of the people, their customary practice and their current position. To seek to foster one of these forms of morale in an unfavorable setting is likely to be fruitless. The methods of cultivating practical morale are likely to be disintegrative in a group which is nurturing a romantic or sacred goal. The methods of romantic and sacred morale are likely to fall flat in a group organized around a goal of essential expediency.

In the light of this discussion we can turn to some consideration of morale in the United States in the present war.

MORALE IN AMERICA

Morale in this country in the present war seems clearly to be of the first type which I have considered—that which is organized around a goal of practical necessity.

The background for our morale was none too propitious. The unfavorable circumstances are still vivid in our memory and so will require little more than mere mention. The organization of our national life on the basis of interest groups exerting constant and numerous pressures would not suggest an easy formation of a joint goal and spirit of co-operation. The existence of conflicts between races, between the native population and minority groups, between labor and industrialists, between various economy blocs, between political groupings, and between alignments on New Deal legislation suggests an unfavorable prospect. The disillusionment following in the wake of the first World War, the presence of a substantial pacifistic philosophy, especially in youths, and the vigorous presentation of a traditional isolationist position were not encouraging factors. The fact that participating in the war had become a bitter issue of the first magnitude indicates further the peculiar background out of which morale would have to be formed. There was practically nothing in the situation that would favor the formation of a romantic or sacred goal. However, the attack on Pearl Harbor following upon an increasing apprehension and suspicion of Axis intentions definitely set our war effort as a matter of practical necessity.

This, I think, represents the state of American attitude and the temper of American feeling with reference to our war effort. We are in the war, and necessity requires us to win it. The typical view is, "Let's get it over with." It is about the only common view and feeling among American people, and it points to a goal of essential expediency. The winning of the war is a terminal end. The effort to get the American people to view this goal in a romantic or sacred way has been markedly unfruitful. The evidence is all too convincing that the American people do not hearken to the urgings that the war should be won to establish a new order of life or to extend and materialize an ideal philosophy. They are not animated by the sense of a cause, of engaging in a crusade, of carrying out a sacred mission; or of affirming new conceptions of themselves in terms of glory, prestige, power, or esteemed position. Scattered voices, to be sure, speak out for such sacred or romantic conceptions, and individuals, here and there, envision such goals. But their views do not seem to represent the way in which the American people sense and feel their objective. For them the winning of the war is a necessary job that has to be done.

In characterizing American morale in this way, there is no impugning of the genuine character of patriotic sentiment. Indeed, it is because of the high value placed on the nation, on what it stands for, and on what it implies in individual life that the winning of the war becomes a matter of practical necessity. There is no question as to the existence of a sense of duty and of a willingness of co-operation. Morale organized around a goal of essential expediency has these features. This type of morale, as suggested in previous remarks, may be exceedingly firm: the spirit of determination may be profound and the spirit of co-operation may be unquestioned. The only point which I wish to stress is that the collective enterprise is organized primarily on the principle of essential and reasoned necessity, and adjustment is made to it chiefly on this basis.

This principle indicates the framework in which morale is formed in this country and sets the line along which conscious efforts to foster morale must move. Fundamentally, the task is that of sustaining the realization that the winning of the war is a necessity and of making and keeping *clear* what is jointly required for this purpose. The generation of emotional enthusiasm, the weaving of a veil of sublimity around the enterprise, the cultivation of myths, or the glorification of gains to be achieved may serve accessory uses, but they do not represent, in my judgment, the central line along which our morale is being formed.

With this understanding of the type of our morale and the principle around which it centers, we can turn to a series of questions, of which the first will be: What is the state of our morale?

The answer to this question is obviously a matter of judgment. So far there are no devices that measure precisely the disposition of people to act together toward a given collective goal. We can only judge this as reasonably as possible.

As we approach this problem it is important to realize a point suggested earlier—that it is possible for a collective enterprise, even of huge dimensions, to be carried on with a minimum of intense attachment to a goal or heightened spirit of co-operation. This may be true in a measure in our country—I do not say that it is true. It is conceivable that our equipment, skills, organization, size, and power are providing a momentum that is carrying on the collective effort without much demand on collective determination or collective support. It is possible, though highly doubtful, that the war might be fought through to a successful conclusion without a high order of morale among people in general. I mention this merely to indicate that the efficiency of collective effort, while it usually points to high morale, is no necessary sign of it. There is always an amount of habituation in a collective enterprise—a participation in the swing of things that is naturally given, and taken for granted, without implying strong collective determination.

Accordingly, the successful carrying-on of joint activity and the signs or indices thereof need not betoken a high order of morale. Purchase of government bonds, liberal contributions to charitable enterprises serving the war, obedience to draft legislation, acceptance of rationing and other restrictions, acceptance of high taxation, increased production and increased conservation—all these are undeniable signs of efficient group functioning but not necessarily of high morale. I wish to be painfully clear here. I do not mean that such activities imply hypocrisy but merely that in themselves they are no certain indication of a strong collective intention to achieve a goal. Nor, as is shortly to be explained, is a deficiency in such activities, under certain circumstances, a sign of low morale.

The real test of morale, as asserted before, is the ability to persist in effort in the face of obstacle and adversity. The demonstrated willingness of the people to endure hardships, suffer deprivations, make sacrifices, and assimilate reversals and still persist in their effort is the true sign of morale. The extent to which the various activities mentioned above—purchase of bonds, etc.—represent significant deprivations and sacrifices, I am not able to judge. Further, it is not possible to say with certainty how willingly the American people would undergo more profound and vital sacrifices as in the case of a lengthy war, or serious defeats of our armed forces, or dubious prospects of victory. Personally, I believe that morale would be high, just as I believe that the various forms of war participation mentioned above do point to a good morale.

I believe this to be so because of the type of morale which we have—that centering around a goal of practical necessity. Much of the indicatory action mentioned—purchase of bonds, acceptance of rationing restrictions, response to draft rules, increased industrial production, etc.—may have occurred as a result of emotional enthusiasm or as mere acquiescence in a collective program. It seems, however, to have arisen much more from a feeling and understanding that it was required in the war effort. It is conceived of, and accepted, in terms of a practical action *necessary* for the winning of the war. Where such realization is made clear there seems to have been successful response. Where demands made on the citizenry are not clearly understood by them as genuinely essential to the war effort, there may be dilatory and unsatisfactory response. It is in this sense that a deficiency of certain kinds of activities such as bond purchase or rationing may indicate not low morale but instead an inability to relate these actions to the sense of required need. My impression is that our people generally respond wholeheartedly to a major demand made of them when its essential necessity to the winning of the war is made clear. I should expect this in view of the generic type of our morale. I suspect that increasing deprivation or adversity would be taken in stride just because of the likelihood that they would yield a more vivid sense of *needed* behavior in the war effort.

To the extent that the appreciation of the necessity of certain actions for the achievement of the goal is not vivid, one may expect a certain amount of opposition, or token adherence, or compromising on the extent of participation. I think that most of us are familiar with this at different points in our own personal lives. We see it in minor evasions of rationing, in the tempering of contributions, and so forth. Without an imminent sense of the practical demands made by the war effort such behavior is not unexpected or to be taken too seriously as signs of poor morale. It is too much to expect people to have an omnipresent sense of the demands required for the winning of the war. There are areas of public life, accordingly, where desired action has to be guided and secured by law and regulation.

Ultimately, the genuine indications of poor morale where it is organized around a goal of practical necessity are clear: an unwillingness on the part of given people to understand what is required of them by the war necessity or, in the face of such an understanding, a refusal to act on the basis of it. Such unwillingness and refusal indicate a divided group, a rejection of the goal of the group enterprise, the absence of co-operative feeling. An inertia, a reluctance, a hesitation, or a failure to act in a required way must be identified as arising from a refusal to understand the importance of what is asked or a refusal to act on such an understanding, before being taken as a sign of poor morale.

In the light of these ideas we can consider briefly some of the things that are regarded usually as the danger spots in our morale situation. One of them is our alien and minority groups: Italians, Germans, Japanese, East Europeans, and Negroes. A full discussion of the position, attitudes, and conduct of such peoples in this country would have to be lengthy. There is no need of it in this paper. Such peoples on the whole have not endangered our morale. Rather, in many ways we have refused them the full co-operation which they have been willing to give; or we have failed to make clear the importance to them of our winning the war and to grant them an opportunity commensurate to this importance. Despite such a degree of failure, such peoples have co-operated and, as far as I can judge, have never constituted any significant threat.

There has been much concern over how American people

would respond to deprivation in the form of rationing, economic dislocation, and taxation. This has been and still is regarded as a source of danger to morale. The evidence from our experience so far is that satisfactory acceptance and adjustment are readily made, once the need of such actions is clearly recognized. I would expect this to be true in the future.

A third danger is presumed to spring from foreign propaganda. This likewise seems to be of little significance. The evidence is quite clear that foreign short-wave broadcasts are listened to by relatively few people, many of whom are animated chiefly by curiosity. Such broadcasts have been declared by some individuals to be the source of rumors and malicious assertions subsequently to be planted in our population by enemy agents. Despite persistent search and interest, I have not been able to get any convincing evidence which would bear out this contention. As far as I can judge, foreign propaganda has not seriously threatened our morale.

A more serious apprehension arises in the case of interest politics and in the operation of strong pressure groups. The picture of the continuing struggles between labor, farmer, and industrialist is disquieting. Strikes, opposition to labor regulation, question of parity prices, pressure for special-interest legislation, the effort to revoke previously enacted laws of welfare, with attendant charge, countercharge, and propaganda, suggest a picture such as Hitler had in mind when he wrote of being able to induce dissension and revolution in this country whenever he wished. Yet, there seems to be no doubt that each major interest and bloc are committed to the winning of the war. The major difficulties seem to arise from a suspicion that one group or the other is seeking to use the war situation to its own advantage—that the winning of the war is to implement a gain by one group at the expense of others. Where such suspicion is absent, co-operation seems to be readily secured. When events occasion a vivid reaffirmation of the need of winning the war, conflict between interest groups seems to subside.

Finally, many thoughtful students are disquieted by the picture of a sizable heterogeneous group suspected to be lukewarm, with attitudes tinged by political bitterness and personal enmity and intrenched in the possession of a significant press. It is felt that this group, keystoned by certain powerful newspapers, is ready to sabotage the war effort when opportunity arises for the satisfaction of personal, clique, and "circle" aims. That there is a certain ground for this apprehension may be true. It seems clear, however, that such a group is controllable by a general attitude in this country of winning the war, that such a group, itself, voices such an endeavor, and that in perilous circumstance where necessity becomes imminent attachment to the war goal would become greater.

In short, it would seem on the whole that American people are united on the basis of winning the war. Their morale remains high and their unity stable to the extent that they believe one another to be seeking this end. The threat to morale seems to arise primarily in suspicions on the part of various groups that others are using the war for special purposes or plan to do so. In a way American morale seems to be in the nature of a *modus operandi* in the face of a crucial need—threats of the violation of such a relation seem to be the chief source of danger to morale.

In my closing remarks I would like to make some general observations. A morale, such as ours, which is formed around a goal of expedient necessity, implies the suspension of previous aims and values rather than their transformation. The aims and values of individual citizens and special groups are subordinated or shelved. The common expression "for the duration" is more than a convenient circumlocution. It is highly symbolic of our psychology. It signifies the thought and expectation of roughly resuming from the point of interruption occasioned by the war. Under such a psychology tensions, conflicts, and cross-strivings are held in abeyance or in check—they are not resolved. Such a condition is to be expected in collective effort directed to a goal of practical necessity and need not be incompatible with a strong morale. However, to the extent that the goal loses its character of essential need, tensions and conflicts may reappear. If the winning of the war comes to be regarded increasingly as certain, as inevitable on the basis of the effort and organization made, there is likely to be a relaxing of felt need and a resurgence of inner conflict and struggle. Such is a danger likely to be encountered by our country. The condition is one wherein victory and success do not lead, as is often asserted, to increased morale. In the study of many groups whose morale has been of the practical sort my impression is that morale has been strengthened by victory up to the point where ultimate achievement is sensed as uncertain; beyond that point continued success, while not leading necessarily to disintegration of collective effort, is likely to lessen the intensity of the morale.

A further thought refers to the post-war situation. In it our morale may be low or nonexistent. By this I mean that we may not be able to form a collective goal of reconstruction which will command a high order of determined effort and co-operative spirit. The existence of a high morale in the war effort is no sign of the retention of such morale in a different undertaking.

My final remark is a sketchy one referring to the transformation of the morale of a people. It should be clear that morale may change as experience leads to a redefinition of the goal. The change may be great enough to transform the fundamental type of morale. It is possible for practical, romantic, and sacred goals to change into one another—but such a transformation requires profound and unusual experience. Whether the shifts, travail, and intensity of our war experience may induce a change in our type of morale, as they have in certain other nations, cannot be foretold. But the possibility should be mentioned. The emergence of a romantic or sacred goal in our country embodying a new dynamic ideal would have profound consequences for the world order after the war.

BIBLIOGRAPHY

American Journal of Sociology, "National Morale," Vol. XLVII, No. 3 (November, 1941).

Annals of the American Academy of Political Science, July, 1941, and March, 1942.

FARAGO, L. *German Psychological Warfare*. New York, 1941.

GILLESPIE, ROBERT D. *Psychological Effects of War on Citizen and Soldier*. New York, 1942.

HALL, G. STANLEY. *Morale: The Supreme Standard of Life and Conduct*. New York, 1920.

HOCKING, WILLIAM E. *Morale and Its Enemies*. New Haven, 1918.

TAYLOR, EDMUND. *The Strategy of Terror*. Boston, 1940.

WATSON, G. B. (ed.). *Civilian Morale*. Boston, 1942.

INDEX

✿

Aged: in agriculture, during present war, 91; in industry, during present war, 73

Agricultural Adjustment Administration, 84

Agricultural Adjustment committees of farmers, 85

Agricultural labor; *see* Farm labor

Agricultural production goals, 86–88

Agricultural surpluses, 83, 84

Agriculture, federal controls over, 83

Aliens, as danger to morale, 227

American agriculture, position of: during first World War, 83; at outset of second World War, 83

American cities: decentralization of, 64; federal relief and reconstruction programs for, 65, 66; rate of growth of, decline in, 63

American Civil Liberties Union, 145

American Legion, 45, 48; attitude of, toward Japanese Americans, 144, 159

American small-towner: satisfaction of, in war, 46; sense of significance of, in wartime, 46

American towns, integration of, through common hatred of common enemy, 47–48; integration of, by war activities, 42, 46–47; social changes in, 40–43; social structure of, complexity of, 44

Army Institute, 112

Associations including all class levels, 45

Atlantic Charter, 133, 165

Automobile transportation, curtailment of: on farms, 103; and its effects, 73–74

Bailey, Thomas Pearce, *Race Orthodoxy in the South*, 175–76

Birth rates: changes in, during first World War, 7–9, 26; changes in, during second World War, 25–26; increase in,

due to war, 6–7, 25–26; natural increase in, during first World War, 9–11

Buck, Pearl S., *Of Men and Women*, 30

Children: in agriculture, in present war, 91; in industry, during present war, 73; neglect of, during wartime, 22

Children's Bureau, 187

Churchill, Winston, 183

Chute, Charles L., 22

Cities; *see* American cities

Citizens: conception of other nations, 128–29; conception of self, 125–27; emotions of, as affected by news, 130; emotions of, as affected by rumors, 132–33; *esprit de corps* of, 122–23; freedom and power of, during wartime, 121–24; habits of, changes in, 124–25; high morale of, 118–19; role of, in total war, 118; unanimity of, in present war, 119–20

Civilian Defense organizations, 74

Class levels of American towns, 44–45

Collective mind, 170, 172

Community organization movement, 74–75

"Conquered Banner, The" (poem), 138–39

Conviction rates: and criminal behavior, 193–97; and public attitude toward crime, 194–95

Convictions: of all classes, 186; by general classes of crimes, 189–90; under highway acts, 196–97; for infractions of special war laws, 191–92; of juveniles, 187–88; for major crimes, 190–91; of men, 186–87; for minor crimes, 190–91; post-war, 191; for sex offenses, 189–90; for thefts, 189, 190, 196; trends in, 185–93; for white collar crimes, 192–93; of women, 187, 188

Co-operative marketing associations among farmers, 83

233